intensive
care

intensive care

more poetry & prose by nurses

Edited by Cortney Davis & Judy Schaefer

University of Iowa Press Ψ Iowa City

University of Iowa Press, Iowa City 52242

Copyright © 2003 by the University of Iowa Press

All rights reserved

Printed in the United States of America

http://www.uiowa.edu/uiowapress

The publication of this book was generously supported by the University of Iowa Foundation.

Printed on acid-free paper

Library of Congress Cataloging-in-Publication Data

Intensive care: more poetry and prose by nurses / edited by Cortney Davis and Judy Schaefer.

p.   cm.

ISBN 0-87745-838-3 (paper)

1. Nurses' writings, American.   2. Nurse and patient—Literary collections.   3. American literature—20th century.   4. Nursing— Literary collections.   5. Nurses—Literary collections.   I. Davis, Cortney, 1945–.   II. Schaefer, Judy, 1944–.

PS508.N87 I58 2003

810.8'092613'09049—dc21   2002075074

03   04   05   06   07   P   5   4   3   2   1

For my husband, Jon, and for those nurses whose stories, for now, remain untold.

C. D.

For my daughter, Jill, my hero, and for the many 24/7 heroes. You know who you are, and you know for what reason.

J. S.

CONTENTS

Foreword

CORTNEY DAVIS

Since our first anthology, *Between the Heartbeats*, was pub-
lished in 1995, there has been a small revolution in nurses' writ-
ing: our poems and stories are now a recognized part of the med-
ical humanities canon and an important addition to literature in
general. The world has changed over the past seven years in other
ways as well. Since September 11, 2001, we've never felt more vul-
nerable, and we've never been more thankful for those who have
our lives in their keeping.

It seems like a perfect time, then, to present this new collection
of creative writing by registered nurses. As co-editors, Judy Schae-
fer and I had the wonderful task of selecting the best of nurses'
writing. It was like choosing from a garden in full bloom. We
could open any issue of the *American Journal of Nursing*, for ex-
ample, and find nurses' well-crafted poems. Many of them are re-
printed here. We surveyed journals and online sites — *Annals of
Internal Medicine*, *JAMA*, *Mediphors*, *Nursing Spectrum*, *NurseZone
.com*, and *RN* — as well as other clinical and literary publications.

We read volumes of poetry and essays, choosing the work of
well-known nurse/writers like Theodore Deppe, Veneta Masson,
Sallie Tisdale, and Belle Waring. We sent out calls for submission,
wondering how managed care and the nursing shortage would
affect nurses' poems and how nurses' stories would reflect recent
cultural, personal, and technological changes. What about the
politics of medicine and the ever-evolving relationship between
doctors and nurses? And, in these uneasy times, what about the
memories of past political conflicts, wars re-revisioned by nurses
who'd been there?

Seldom sentimental, sometimes controversial, our final selec-
tion of poems, stories, and personal essays conveys the range of
emotions we nurses juggle as we go about our work: love, fear,
gratitude, frustration, fatigue, transcendence, grace. We included
writing by women and men from a variety of nursing backgrounds
and from a wide geographic distribution — the United States
(from Florida to Alaska), Canada, England, Ireland, Hungary,

Brazil, and Nicaragua. Much of what nurses have to say in this new volume reinforces the positive messages of *Between the Heartbeats*: we nurses care tenderly and passionately about our profession and our patients; we are able to stand by and comfort the suffering and the dying; we cherish, most of all, the opportunity to accompany patients along the path to healing.

Many of the topics in this volume are new. Amy Haddad and Janet Bernichon write about being patients themselves, on the other side of surgery, cancer, and the experience of chemotherapy. Nurses who have lost parents, grandparents, or partners write about the difficulty of assuming the dual roles of child and nurse, or lover and caregiver. Some, like Ruth Brooks, write about earlier days of nursing education and practice. Others write about how their grandmothers — with white stockings, stiff caps, and moral determination — influenced their own careers. You'll find nurses like Janet Tripp and Marlene Cesar, who speak out against the rushed, mechanized, callous moments in health care, and nurses like Pamela Mitchell and Paula Sergi, who write about why and how an RN might both love and leave the profession.

In these pages, we also reveal ourselves as wholly human, celebrating the reality of the flesh as well as the spirit. Miriam Bruning Payne writes about how making love helps us transition from work to home; in one way or another, she suggests, all of us long to witness love daily. Madeleine Mysko and Jessica Shrader dare to mention nontraditional couples, a tenderness and commitment that the rest of the world often ignores, while Constance Studer risks writing about what happens when nurses make mistakes, how grief compounds grief when work and personal loss intertwine.

As they did in *Between the Heartbeats*, nurses write about birth and, more often, about death. Perhaps the specter of death lurks in everything we do. While this may dismay some readers — I'd ask those individuals to seek out the many joyful or humorous stories and poems here — others might find comfort in the details of nurses' attentiveness, our proximity to the mysteries of life's beginnings and endings. Readers who are nurses, especially, may take comfort in knowing that their moments alone with the newly born and the dying are recognized here for what they are: privileged, frightening, rewarding, blessed.

In this collection, we again present the authors alphabetically, letting their voices unfold as they will, rather than artificially dividing the book into sections. Those who read from beginning to end will find some happy accidents: Sandra Bishop Ebner's poem "The Shape of the Human Spine" is followed a few pages later by Maureen Flannery's "Rubbing Her Back at the Nursing Home." Then there's Robin Chard's simple, sweet poem about OR nurses followed by Victoria Collett's "The Color of Blood," a piece that lifts the mask to reveal another point of view.

Readers might also notice how even the most serious poems utilize rhymes and rhythms that mimic the blood *swoosh*, the birth contraction, the cycle of a life. Perhaps it seems odd to mix illness with such music, but our work — our intensive caregiving — is made up of just such wondrous contradictions.

Welcome to this new anthology. We hope it pleases, stirs, and amazes you.

intensive care

Medical Ward

KRYSTINA AHLMAN *Milton, Vermont*

someone asked me once
            why be a nurse

I stood leaning against the ward's tiles
            feeling the cool of their sticky yellow
            feeling the ache of my feet

the shift was almost over
charting would keep me late again
I was wearing a thousand tiny failures

an old man died today
his wife stayed with him
until he was quite cold

two worn parents
watched their drunken daughter
wet herself
            and vomit on my shoes

I tipped the faded bedside roses

the husband with the cancer-ridden wife called me a bitch
instead of crying into his hands

fierce courageous love
crowds
into small rooms

awash in ugliness
            pain
            self-destruction and rage

there is always a flotsam
            of spirit

I held out my hand, I said
I am not afraid to cry

A Moment in the History of Nursing

FRANCES MURPHY ARAUJO
North Weymouth, Massachusetts

Colleen was a baby—fifteen months old, failure to thrive. When we admitted her to Pediatrics, it was evident she had an old head injury. We suspected she'd been abused, although it was not so common then. Back then we were still shocked. Colleen's head was irregular in shape, and soft as a melon gone to rot—like if you pressed the skin too hard, your finger would break through the skin to the orange mushy flesh. I was frightened by the feel of her head. It was the first time I had seen a child with that kind of damage. I sensed danger. I felt breathless.

Usually, Baby Colleen lay quite still in her crib, except for little startles. She stared up at the ceiling with her pale eyes focused on nothing. I wondered if she was blind. When I was bathing her, I noticed that her legs didn't feel right either—knotty under the flesh, not smooth like a baby's limbs should be. Later, when we took X rays, we discovered all the old healed fractures that never set properly and were never treated.

Colleen was my patient, my assignment, and it was because of that randomness and because of the choices I was able to make in my nursing care that the moment happened.

I took her in my arms, careful to steady her head. I held her against me. She was small and scrawny and didn't have the solid, sturdy feel of a normal baby. I didn't feel within her that sense of energy I always look for, that "otherness," that life force you feel under your hands when you touch another. That mystery that says "Here I am" seemed to be gone. This baby was broken.

I'd been taking care of people all my life, and I had seen the body's amazing ability to heal, but this was new to me. The damage done to Colleen—inflicted by those entrusted with her care—filled me with fear. Gooseflesh. Couldn't get the air into my lungs. They ruined her. I believed I was close to evil. I was face to face with it. It was so ordinary, yet so deep; it terrified me.

I did the only thing I could think of. I bundled Colleen against me and sat in the rocking chair, and we rocked. I rocked the two of us. Back and forth. Rocked and rocked. Back and forth. Luckety-luck, back and forth. Pushing my feet against the floor, feeling them lift, airborne, as we went back. Down again. Push again. The rockers made that luckety sound on the gray tile floor. It was like being on a swing. Or on a big swooping bird. Baby Colleen and I, riding a bird. I held her firmly. I put one hand under her skinny little bottom and one on the base of her downy little mush-melon head. I breathed in her faint powdery smell, and we rocked. Colleen and I. I talked softly into her ear. Sweet little girl, I said. Colleen. God's own little child. I said what I would later say to my own children, when they came into the world. I sang into her ear. A made-up song:

> Luckety-luck,
> Little girl.
> God's gonna take you
> From this world.

I sang with the rhythm of the rockers. For that moment we were free, both of us, lifted by the sound of my voice, the rockers, the whoosh of the oxygen in the tents, the slide of the metal crib rails going up and down, the soft padding of the nurses' shoes on the floor, the swish of nylon uniforms, even the page system calling for stat lab techs and Code Blue.

It seemed a great humming was all around us. There we were in the middle, both of us needing something. I soothed us the best way I knew, in a rocking chair. It was natural. Most babies like rocking and singing. You feel them burrow into your neck a little deeper. They sigh or turn their heads. I've seen babies, even the tiniest, make a sound, maybe a little squeak, as if they were trying to join in the singing. At first Baby Colleen didn't do any of that. She was still, except for those jerky movements with the sudden clenching and opening of her small fists, as if she were receiving little electrical shocks.

I was afraid, but I closed my eyes and kept rocking and humming, and finally I felt something coming from her. Something happened. As we rocked, she got warmer. A rise in body temperature. The subtlest change. A slight shift in weight. A feathery quiet breath on my neck. Deep inside, maybe she knew she was safe for that moment, and she wanted to let me know. We were joined, and it helped us both.

I believe in certain things: that we live each other's lives, and

that we belong to one another. And I believe that all human be-
ings, given enough time, will move toward love. I believe that
every life, no matter how brief or how long or how complicated
it looks on the outside, is, in its own way, perfect. It was that
moment with Baby Colleen that fostered that faith. I thank her
for that.

Night Shift

JANE BAILEY *Salem, Oregon*

"How much longer?" the mother asked
and we told her

as nurses we were not allowed
to predict or diagnose.

Then the father asked, "How long?" absentmindedly
crushing the empty nest of a farmer's cap in his hands.

The mother stuck a finger through
a tear in her son's motorcycle jacket

and said, "He was on his way home
to help us harvest the wheat."

They stood in the tireless fluorescent light
as straight and as terrible as the couple in *American Gothic*,

watching the steady row of waves crossing
the heart monitor. How much longer could it go on?

When we finally relented and offered an hour, maybe four,
we could see how grateful they were to know, to be so close

to the end, and they stood at the bedside until 3 A.M.
when we turned the monitor off.

September

JANE BAILEY *Salem, Oregon*

Today I've decided to stop looking
for more beautiful things to break.
I won't even glance at the horizon,
which is always about separation.

I'm just going to walk on the beach
and hum with the waves, which are also humming
Whitman's song — *we are one, we are one* —
while someone else's small white dog

goes hoarse chasing the tide, and the wind
continues its business of ruffling the dead
feathers, twisted birds, and cracked shells,
then setting them down for gulls to pick over.

Maybe I'll close my eyes and lie down
on the sand while the sun works its miracle
on a sky so blue it's as if there had never been
clouds or fog, or the thought of clouds or fog.

There will be a happy ending. Finally,
after all the sad poems. No boys will succumb
to the undertow or be picked off by sneaker waves.
No girls will trip over driftwood logs.

Later, perhaps, I'll tell you about
a different day on the same beach at Road's End,
and I'll be the hero of that poem, too,
though the details will be grimmer.

For instance, things I overlooked here
will have to be described in detail:
There was a steep rock cliff
and a young man who climbed it, drunk.

His girlfriend looked like a cartoon girl
sprinting toward me on the beach, calling
for help. It will be important to know
that I am a nurse and I run five miles a day

which is just long enough to forget a night
of resuscitations and Code Blues.
In that poem, I'm still slender and childless
so I'll want to mention my nipples, how pink they were,

how they perked up in the wind
when I took off my green Death Valley t-shirt
and stanched the fallen man's bleeding head.
Some readers will naturally turn toward sex

when I juxtapose my white breasts
with the dark blue crotch of the man's wet jeans.
There may be a few nervous laughs
when I say that the surf repeatedly licked

the man's legs and testicles, so when I asked him
do you know what day this is, all he'd say
to me and his girlfriend and a balding fiftyish man
who stood back and tried not to look at my breasts

was, "My balls! O, my balls!" And of course
you'll want to know he survived. The Life Flight
helicopter took off. The tide found its way back out.
I put on someone's scratchy sweater.

The saltwater took every red stain out
of my shirt, but I gave it away to Goodwill
the next week. We all went on with our lives.
We took children to the beach

and watched them only about half the time.
We stopped looking for blood on the rocks.
You see, we all went on living, and
that's where I'd want any poem to end.

Thin Margin

CAROL BATTAGLIA *Brookfield, Illinois*

The only thing
that separates us
is that I have not
yet been diagnosed.

The Dance

ANDREA LEE BELIVEAU *British Columbia, Canada*

To partner with a stranger
in a dance
where two can lead
a nurse steps onto the dance floor
      training ear for rhythm change
      humming over grumbly cello notes
      balancing thundering cymbals

To partner with a stranger
in a dance
a nurse tunes in
to meaningful notes
      practicing the art of nursing
      matching the technical tones

Does This Date Mean Anything to You?

LYNN BERNARDINI *Oxford, Connecticut*

Twenty-three years ago, long before I became a registered nurse and began working in a neonatal intensive care unit, I gave my newborn son up for adoption.

My relationship with the baby's father was insignificant. We were both young and carefree, living only for the moment in the time of Woodstock, flower children, and the Vietnam War — certainly we were not suited for a lifelong relationship. But in 1970, unwed mothers were scorned, and homes for such mothers were common. When my parents learned of my pregnancy and my refusal to marry the baby's father, I was sent away.

Because living at the "Home" would be very expensive, I opted for my parents' less costly counter offer: I would live with a family and work for them, babysitting and housekeeping. A nineteen-year-old immature teenager, I was away from home for the first time, and strange things were happening to my body. The family was pleasant enough, the work was fair, and the kids were good. But I had shamed my parents, I was estranged from my friends, I was alone. And soon I would be abandoning my child.

I couldn't even do pregnancy correctly. Swollen, tired, and finally, toxic with severe preeclampsia, I had to be hospitalized. The doctors told me I might die; even then, I didn't care. Fortunately, I met a social worker at the hospital clinic — she became my angel — and there was one OB nurse who really cared. These women talked to me, always remaining supportive and professional. But none of my family members came to visit. None of my friends were allowed to know. I had no significant other who cared. In two days, when I was discharged back to my "family," I realized that it was really just me and my baby — I had no one to cry to but him. I swore that he was not going to suffer for my mistakes.

A few mornings after my hospitalization, my contractions started. At first I couldn't figure out what was happening — before this I'd only guessed what labor might be like. I tiptoed downstairs from my room and left a note on the kitchen table, hoping the woman of the family I lived with would find it. "After your kids and your husband are off in the morning," I wrote, "please come check on me and bring me back to the hospital." Sure enough, I would give birth eighteen hours later, but my temporary "mother" said she couldn't stay with me. Her kids were due home at 3 P.M.

Do you have any idea what labor feels like to a teenager in a room all alone? A nurse comes in for two minutes once a hour. There's nothing to do but lie on your back staring at a clock. A resident comes to check on you every two or three hours, asking the same monotone questions. When it gets dark outside, the demons of *Beowulf* come out: Women scream, people run, babies cry. I tried to breathe correctly, as I had learned in the classes that were given to us unwed mothers, but we'd also been told that true Lamaze wasn't possible. After all, they'd said, the fathers weren't involved, and a mother couldn't do Lamaze by herself. Now that I'm a nurse, I'm a strong believer: No one should ever go through the birth process alone.

As I labored, I heard fathers making happy phone calls in the hall. Nurses kept calling me by my mother's name, as if I were married. I just wanted them to call me by my first name. I wanted someone to be nice to me, rather than scowling every time they came into my cubicle. I didn't ask for anything; I thought if I was quiet and good, the nurses would like me. I only wanted some ice or to have someone sit by me in the chair. I hurt inside, I hurt outside. I hurt in my soul. But I was a clinic patient, not happily married and so, I told myself, I was getting what I deserved. Shame on me. This was the price I had to pay.

Of course, my water couldn't break when the resident was in the room. It broke when I was alone, and by the time someone answered my call bell, my knees were up and the baby's head was out. I heard nurses' voices yelling *Don't push, don't push* and felt someone shoving an anesthesia mask over my face as my stretcher was being pushed down the hall into a bright room. Then a doctor I'd never seen before was standing over me in a strange corridor and asking, "Why do you women always have to have babies so fast in the middle of the night?"

He'd delivered my baby boy, he explained, but he wasn't my doctor. And he advised me not to look at or hold my son. "It will be better that way. Just get back to your life, and I'll see you next year to do this all over again. Ladies like you always come back."

That morning I called the family I was staying with. I didn't phone my mother until late that afternoon; then all I said was, "It's over."

My hospital social worker came to visit and brought me an inexpensive bracelet made of violets — a gift, she said, from my son. She told me where my baby was if I wanted to see him. I did, and so we took that long walk.

He was in the nursery, over in the corner away from the viewing window with a sign on his bed: Do Not Show. The social worker, my angel, brought him to the window and unwrapped him. He was whole, beautiful, blond. He looked just like me. And he was just as alone. I knew what was right for him. I knew I was not to be his mother. I only wanted to hold him and hug him once to say good-bye.

My angel said she would be back the next day to bring me into the nursery to hold him, but I never saw her again. Overnight, I'd been assigned a new social worker who agreed with the doctor that I shouldn't see or hold my baby, that I should consider him dead.

I snuck back to the nursery twice. The first time I saw my baby alone, highlighted by the sun as if something from beyond was watching over him. The next time, he was gone. My arms would never hold or hug him. I'd never be able to ask him to understand or to forgive me.

I stayed with my assigned family for another month. When it was time for me to go home, I'd been away six months. I still have no idea where I was supposed to have been for that amount of time; my parents never said what they had told the neighbors. And no one asked.

Eight weeks later, my angel sent me the hospital birth certificate — my only keepsake and the only proof that my baby really existed. No pictures. No warm fuzzy blanket. No memories.

It took me years to like myself, to decide I was a good person, to understand that postpartum depression happens even when you don't bring a baby home. No one discussed any of this with me because, technically, I didn't *have* a baby. To most people, I had simply been on vacation.

For twenty-three years, I wondered. What ever happened to him? Where was he? Was he happy? Was he alive? What was he like? Every time I heard about a child being abducted, abused, or killed, I would think, *It could be him.*

In 1974, I married my friend and soul mate who knew all about my child. He understood that I would never go looking for this lost-to-me child. I'd given him life so he could make someone else's life whole. I wasn't going to ruin that by unexpectedly popping into his life.

"But," I told my husband, "if this child finds me, you'll have to accept him as you've accepted me."

"No problem," he said. He loved me.

Nevertheless, I worried that if I got pregnant again, some divine intervention might pay me back for what I'd done. When I did get pregnant, I worried the whole nine months. Would I have a miscarriage? Would I ever have another son? I had abandoned my firstborn and that made me, I once believed, a bad person. But lives change. Now I have a healthy family, a home, a career in a busy neonatal intensive care unit where I help other women's babies survive. I'm very good at what I do. And my husband and I have three sons: our own two and a special friend.

In August, 1992, I received a phone call from an agency in New Haven.

"Does June 2, 1970, mean anything to you?" a woman asked. I hesitated for a long time. After all, this was a date I'd been told to forget by the judge when I'd signed the final adoption papers. That date meant everything to me, but society didn't want me to recognize it. How could I admit out loud to the stranger on the phone that my world had changed that day in 1970? I had grown up that day. I had become a mother that day, a hidden-away teenager who disgraced her family. That's the day every year that I cried uncontrollably. But no one was supposed to know.

"Does that date mean anything to you?" the voice repeated. If that call meant what I thought it meant, did I really want this? Did I want to explain my disgrace to my teenage sons? Would this be a reason for others to blame me more than I'd blamed myself?

"Yes," I whispered to the stranger on the phone. "Yes, my wish has come true. On that date, I gave birth to a son."

Phyllis, the agency representative, explained that my son wanted to contact me. Two months later, I received a letter in which my son introduced himself and gave me a short history of his life. At last I knew: He was alive.

We met for the first time in May, 1993, just after Mother's Day. Fear of the unknown made me more nervous that day than on any other day in my life. Once again, I had to do this alone. We both had to do this alone.

I arranged to arrive at the restaurant first. My signal to him was that I would be reading a book. It was a good book — it helped me calm down. In fact, it was so good I suddenly realized there was a pair of shoes standing by my table. Then I heard my name. This is it, I said to myself. Is he going to hate me, yell at me? What will he think of me?

I looked up to meet my son, my adult son. To my delight, he brought pictures from his mother, and I was able to watch him grow up in front of me. The similarities in our lives were eerie. His mother is a nurse. My husband and his father work for the same company. He has a sister with my first name. My husband and I once thought about buying a house down the street from his house. These facts — how close our lives had been all along — gave us chills.

We talked and laughed for a few hours. We agreed to keep in touch. And I finally got to give him a hug. It felt so good, that twenty-three-year-old touch. It had sparks.

When I told my children that they had a half brother, they accepted the news and couldn't wait to meet him. They told all their friends, and I too could at last speak out about a subject that had been taboo. I showed pictures to everyone: A twenty-three-year-old, a seventeen-year-old, and a fourteen-year-old, all going their own directions with their own lives, all their lives a part of mine.

I've explained to my two children that I am Bill's biological mother but not his mom, knowing they might not understand until they have children of their own. The wonderful lady who wanted him as much as I did, who was there for him through the good times, the bad times, and the sick times, is his mother. He turned out to be a good person, so I know she was a wonderful mother, comfortable enough with his love to guide him back to me.

I'd thought, after all these years, that attitudes toward mothers who opted for adoption had changed. But recently, after seeing how one teenage mom in our hospital was treated when she gave up her baby, my nightmares returned. Giving your baby away — a part of yourself — is a major decision, ideally made after much thought and consultation, both before and after the delivery. Holding the infant won't change a mother's mind. Taking pictures of her baby or having a lasting memento won't either. Some mothers need to smell, kiss, touch, and cry over their infants before they can let them go. They may want keepsakes, something to hold on to and look at in the days to come.

Knowing what I went through as a young unwed mother makes me kinder and more supportive of women who make the same difficult decision I made. And I know I've been blessed: I'm not his real mother, I'm his friend, the one who gave him life. But photos of my grown-up, adopted-away son now sit on my windowsill. I have his hugs every time we see each other. Knowing he won a "Beautiful Baby" contest makes me proud. Seeing how, growing up, he looked like my sons, makes me content. Noticing the family resemblance now among my sons warms my heart.

It's as if all the pieces have come together at last.

Object of Desire

JANET BERNICHON *Shirley, New York*

How smoothly the cancer seduces the body.

Lying in the tub, head resting
on the cool porcelain edge
I wash with the same stroke
the same swipe of hand, only now
the rhythm is slower.

The evening before surgery
stepping out of my bath,
I memorized the slick of oil
over the curve of my breasts,
the symmetry in the mirror,
nipples hard, roughened by the towel
like the touch of a lover.
Everything normal

on the surface. No
signs of nature's dirty trick
buried in the fatty tissue
spreading its hold, rooting
into my flesh. My flesh,
its object of desire.

Now, a solo globe is buoyant
in the water's warm mouth.
A red line covers my heart.
My torso winks at me
in that same mirror
as I dry off, my nipple hard.

How smoothly the body seduces the mind.

Chemo

JANET BERNICHON *Shirley, New York*

In the waiting room —
the contradiction of healthy
hair over pallor
or turbans tied with the perfection
that comes with practice
and no one is fooled
by the kid with the shaved head
he's one too, part of the legion
getting on with everyday routines
and being here has become routine.

Amid the muted shades of gray
we mingle small talk
with our collective war story. We gather
like relatives at a wedding
or wake, embracing each other
in our armor plate hope,
buffed daily to a high gloss.

Look.
I can adjust my wig
in its reflection.

Sunday

JANET BERNICHON *Shirley, New York*

working double shift in the Emergency Room,
the day going like a free clinic
in the junkie heartland, everybody strung out
and hurting when someone shouts
"Hey, could you check this chain saw injury?"
that was tourniqueted with a red bandanna
on a blue collar leg,
tan and tight and gashed to the bone.
The rest followed
by-the-book protocol,
closed, patched, expert repairs
with minimal blood loss.
Good-bye. Good luck. Dinner time.

On the 6 o'clock line, I hear it.
A sparrow screeches,
trapped in the air vent
out of reach
                    over the steamed baked ziti.
"We can't get it out," says the cook,
as the tinny rustle of wings against metal
resonates from the shaft.
"What'll it be?"

I say nothing,
appetite killed, caught up
in silent prayers, promises
to God — not to complain, ever again,
about anything —
if he will let that bird
find a way out.

Mercy and Hemlock

JANET BERNICHON *Shirley, New York*

It's 7:55.
At 8 o'clock, comfortable,
we'll make you comfortable
and pull the plug
because you
living-willed life with support
as no life at all.

My gut throbs
because you don't believe
in miracles, just
want the quick, clean, and easy.

Held in strong arms until it's limp,
a rabid dog is put down.

Your misery of tubes
will end tidily and legally.
They will say it's merciful.

A nuisance cat is explained away
to a child who continues to look for it.

You health-care-proxied your wishes,
all of them reasonable.
They will say it's for the best

and was your choice.

Choice, with its back against the wall
holds out a cup of hemlock
and your life ends,

it's 7:56,
in minutes
in minutes

Code Blue

JANET BERNICHON *Shirley, New York*

the center
of strangers
oxygen death masked
wax effigy
mottled, matted
with blood
the only part of you
recognizable
your puffy feet
with their outward
rotation
and even they
are strapped
to some machine

the rest is rigid
rocked with the rhythm
of palms pumping
your heart
the crunch of squab
bones, brittle
wishbone snapping
strangers keep time
and stand clear
of joules
that jerk your arms
upward to unknown

gods
reaching through
white light
to push you back

can you hear me?

Daddy?

Burn

HANNE DINA BERNSTEIN *Brookline, Massachusetts*

His face sooty and distended,
eyes, two blinded domes.
Scattered islands of
frizzled hair and beard
choked in the smell of keratin.
In my sterile green, I lower
his stretcher into the bathtub.
Through my gloves,
I feel his wooden arms.
The disinfectant washes off red.
When I put a razor to his face,
he feels no pain.
When I place a toothbrush in a hand
that has no skin,
he begins to brush his teeth.

Down the Hospital Corridor

HANNE DINA BERNSTEIN *Brookline, Massachusetts*

A hesitant wave of a hand
eyes trying to catch mine
the sound of a throat being cleared
the way it has to be before saying
something personal
something painful.

If I keep my speed
look straight ahead
I can ignore the shame.

I know what they want
cannot be said
in five minutes.
I know compassion
takes fifteen minutes
or more.

Dar a Luz

KIRSTIN BORTZ *Pernambuco, Brazil*

After many adventures in Africa, including helping at a maternity clinic in Mozambique, I arrived here in Brazil where I work as a community health nurse as well as with a variety of women's and youth groups, creating opportunities for participants to explore issues such as gender, women's health, sexuality, and self-esteem. Together, we work to demystify what their society says is right, recreating a new reality in which all have worth and opportunity. During one women's group discussion, I asked everyone to hunt for a symbol that represented to them what it meant to be a woman. My own choice was a candle — to me, being a woman is like being a light. Since I have discovered who I am, what my gifts are, I must help others discover their own. Dar a luz means to give birth — literally, to give light. I can't think of a greater pleasure than helping a woman discover her value, her place, and her gifts, and encouraging her as she brings forth new life.

There was an indescribable energy in the room:
The expectation. The waiting.
Watching her work, sweat, strain.
Holding my breath and pushing along with her.
Seeing that face emerge, seeing it move, fighting for life.
Suddenly one shoulder, then the next!

You, woman, can be cherished.
You, woman, are a precious gift.

Tell me where it hurts.
Take my hand.
Take my hand and place it where it hurts.
Take my hand so I can join you on your difficult journey.
Trust me.
Tell me. I will stop and listen.

I may not understand all your words, your culture.
I may not understand how you can let him dictate your comings

and goings.
I don't understand how he can beat you and treat you like an
    animal.
But I know you can do this.
You can give light.

Uncross your arms!
Unplug your ears!
Listen to your body.
You know your body well.

You will know when it is time to push,
when it is time to relax.

Squat, if your body wants to squat.
I will support you.
Your body knows what is right.
I will massage where it hurts.
I will be right alongside you.

Her heart is beating strong and clear!
These months of preparation are coming to an end!

Let her come!
Dar a luz, dar a luz

what a beautiful light you have brought into this world.

Male Nurse Washing a Nun

GEOFFREY BOWE *Kent, England*

Today
he had washed a nun.
She didn't seem to mind
because he was doing his job.
Her body
looked pale and unused,
her nipples
like the pile of stones
found at the summit of mountains.
He talked to her
about *The Sound of Music*
as he washed her thighs.
"I know all the songs," she said.
He asked her to roll over
so that he could wash her back and bottom
as they discussed Mother Teresa.
For ten minutes
the sponge licked at her body
as a ray of light
entered like an angel
through the gap in her curtains,
illuminating the bed and its contents.
The male nurse noticed
how the pattern on the curtains
looked like stained glass,
her bedside table like an altar.
He found himself kneeling
down, beside the bed,
before pulling himself together
and leaving.

Dark Lines and Words

GEOFFREY BOWE *Kent, England*

"Paint me"
said the patient.
"Show the world
what you see.
Tell them
of my aches and pains,
the problems
I face,
being old.
Show me
as I am.
Paint me in gray
and reveal
my dark lines."

"I am a poet"
said the nurse,
"I shall paint you
with words.
You shall have your gray
and your dark lines.
I will show
your true colors."

Pick Up the Spoon

GEOFFREY BOWE *Kent, England*

You flicker
like a faulty striplight
and mumble
words
which mean nothing anymore.
You sit
in a faded dress
and are fed
by whomever
will pick up the spoon.
You recognize love
and respond to kindness
and at night time
listen
to the sound of your heart.
Loud
in the silence.
Sometimes,
missing a beat.

The Essence of Nursing: 1967

RUTH E. BROOKS *Washington, D.C.*

To My Dear Students,

Who is more alone than a high school senior from Harlem sitting in a dreary library in New England pondering her future? One gray day, I sat with books piled high before me. I read about many fields of work; however, none seemed right for me. Now and then, I'd find something I liked about a career, but there always seemed to be some negative aspect which canceled it out as a possibility. Obtaining the basic necessities for day-to-day survival was my family's unrelenting struggle; I could not contemplate seriously an education that would require huge financial sacrifice. Whatever I decided upon would have to demand only a small initial investment.

That gloomy day, my mood vacillated between unbearable anxiety and marked apathy. Somewhat obsessively, my attention kept coming back to nursing. The nursing schools I read about promised room and board at a nominal cost, a varied social life, supervised experience, and a career that would always be in demand despite the upsurge in automation. Utopia, I thought. Here was an unbelievably simple solution to my problem. I would return home and become a nurse. I would go back to the arms of my first love: Harlem.

Almost as if to reinforce the wisdom of my decision, my father became acutely ill. Although he'd managed to adjust to diabetes and two strokes, now, overpowered, he suffered a third and final one. In the days before his death, I had many opportunities to regret my ignorance of simple home nursing. Love and good intentions, I learned painfully, were not enough. There were skills and techniques that could have relieved my father's distress, but I did not yet possess them. The daughter he loved stood helplessly by or administered clumsily to his needs. When the end came, I watched solemnly and renewed my vow to become a nurse.

At the time, I didn't know any nurses. When I set out to talk to some, I found their answers superficial and evasive. *What is it that you do?* I asked them. *What is the most rewarding part of your career?*

What do you love most about nursing? How do you help patients while maintaining your own health and peace of mind? Now, after graduating and working as a registered nurse for almost eight years, I understand why they were so inarticulate.

Nursing is a most intimate experience. It has brought me a sense of deep and lasting happiness, one that comes from the knowledge that I have helped allay the suffering of countless others. Nursing is the opportunity to be needed, wanted, and loved by total strangers and to need, want, and love them in return. Nurses are blessed with the unique chance to become immortal — patients often tell their families about "the nurse who. . . ." If you do not believe that patients remember you long after their crises have past, let me relate an experience a now middle-aged man shared with me.

One spring, many years ago, while alone in a distant land, he became ill and was hospitalized. Visitors streamed in and out to see all the other patients, intensifying his loneliness and despair. A nurse came over and sat by his bed. "Mr. Gomez," she said softly. "Today is Mother's Day, and you are far from home. So for today, *I'll* be your mother."

Thinking of this nurse and her simple act of tenderness — as he had done so often through his life — he could only say to me, "Imagine. She stayed with me so I wouldn't be afraid. Isn't that something?"

Nursing is also a maturing experience. If nurses have any prejudices, they will relinquish most of them fairly early in their careers, finding that all people suffer, no matter what they believe, how they look, or what language they speak. The realities of life touch us all. I often find that my faith in mankind is revitalized when I see people who were previously strangers giving and receiving care. When I wish for a better world, it is out of the deep conviction that there can be one; as a nurse, I've seen the possibilities that emerge when we become each others' keepers.

Nursing has its rewards. Patients give us tokens of gratitude as if they were sacred offerings. I will always remember the day a patient who spoke no English held out eight glasses she had hand-painted for me, and I'm still amused when I recall a little girl who offered me, with measles-speckled hands, one of her gingersnap cookies. But the gifts I cherish most are not material.

There was a woman with gray-streaked hair who'd recently

suffered a stroke. Her speech was unintelligible and her muscles uncoordinated. I was doing private duty, and she was my patient. The night was cruelly long for her. When morning finally came and it was time for me to go, she wept with frustration because she could not say "Thank you." Instead, she simply pressed my hand to her tear-streaked face, a beautiful way to be thanked.

I recall a night I sang lullabies to an old man who could not sleep. When hot milk, bed baths, massage, and sleeping pills had failed, I tapped my last resource; we both enjoyed those unorthodox hours. I also remember caring for a two-pound infant for several uncertain months. When the family was finally able to take their baby home, the child's mother held my hand for a very long moment to say a special good-bye. The touch of a grateful hand is the most precious gift of all.

There are also times when a nurse goes home carrying the sadness of the day. I recall the gray eyes of a young mother who knew she was dying of cancer even as she listened to her son talk about what they would do tomorrow, his chatter filled with optimism and unreasoned faith. There is an awful uncertainty about tomorrow for the dying patient: it may be the day that is filled with anguish.

Perhaps because nurses deal with such sorrows, we sometimes seem callous, portrayed as rushing about aggressively armed with a hostile hypodermic needle. Behind this image is the real nurse who longs for her patient's recovery. Every day, a nurse is caught up with life and its many problems. Often, the nurse is called upon to be sister, mother, father, physiologist, best friend. Hidden behind our faces, our uniforms, our words, is an identity which emerges out of patients' individual needs. My favorite role has been that of surrogate mother. I've long since lost count of the number of my children, some of them deaf, blind, mentally or physically impaired, premature, delinquent, psychotic, abandoned, or simply recovering from a broken leg. They were black, white, yellow, and brown. Some called me Mrs. Brooks or even Mr. Brooks. Some simply called me *Mama*.

For the most part, I've focused on bedside nursing because it happens to be my primary interest; however, it's only one of the many fields you might choose. You may want to work within the structured environment of a doctor's office, or perhaps you are distressed about the growing numbers of the mentally ill. Maybe you are fascinated by the drama of the operating room. If you'd rather stroll a boulevard in Paris, cruise in a gondola in Venice, savor an exotic dish in the Far East, or marvel at the beauty of Africa, you may be the nurse that airline companies, public health agencies, the armed forces, or the Peace Corps want. And we desperately need men in nursing. In pediatrics, many children need the strong presence of a surrogate father. In medicine and surgery, we need men to offer their steady sympathy and understanding as well as their intelligence.

For the person who thrives on a variety of experiences and needs close contact with others on a meaningful level, there is no greater, no more essential, career to pursue. I promise that if you become a nurse, as I did, you will never suffer from the disease of alienation that has afflicted many members of modern society.

Many years from now when I am old, dear students, I may forget your names, but I will always remember each of you. Meeting you, teaching you, and getting to know you has been one of the greatest joys of my personal and professional life. The experience of nursing will reveal your capacity to love, to give, and to receive. May it bring you bountiful rewards and endless blessings.

The Crickets Went On Singing

CELIA BROWN *Falmouth, Massachusetts*

I remember the night you told me
about the star-fish in your breast.
In the fire's eye I saw it flutter-kick,
how fear sat in the margin of your look,
how you stunned it to the coals,
how it sundered in your limbs.

Grandma, the day the train
took you away,
the crickets went on singing.
Over the fields they quavered,
numbing the rawbone rain.
Everything else was out of tune
with the living: the day you left
you wore your bluebell coat —
a blush of scarf.

I found you after half a summer,
outdoors in the hospital garden,
the crickets sang their loudest tune.
You were frail as Belleek
except for your smile,
while Charity Nuns bloomed
at your side in out-of-season
Easter-lily hats.

Winter brought you home
without a miracle.
The crickets slept — the days
began to fall like dominoes,
we knelt on kitchen chairs,
we filled the house with rosaries —
and you there always lying
in your upstairs room.

Grandma, at the end
if a wish had been a wand,
or a puff upon a string,
I'd have floated you full sun
past the cricket tune of no more
sorrowing: in dreams I see you yet,
and I hear the crickets singing;
your smile half-crazed before you forgot.

Forget-Me-Nots

CELIA BROWN *Falmouth, Massachusetts*

Stork stories notwithstanding, close watching
was believing. I'd know things by the baby
blankets airing, the midnight cough of Mother's
doctor leaving, a gauzy shoal of nappies in the wind.

Meanwhile as Grandma pressed the matinee coats
and Daddy manned the kettles, I'd come to love
the panic of the season, predictable as Creeping
Periwinkle or Nurse O'Mally's blowzy visitations

(small midwife in reserve, my future dreamy,
I'd grow up to be like her with my head draped
in a diaper, a towel around my middle)

All this around the riddle of the War. All ten
of us like myrtle on the gable; year after year.
As if someone had left us too many flowers:
Lily-Turf, Sage, Blue-Eyed Mary.

I sat on the margin of nineteen fifty-two,
star-witness like no other; nine lives piled up
on mine, not all at once but creeping; nine others

to be coddled or ignored like blue Forget-Me-
Nots I'd carry home to Mother; pure, malleable

and sweet, whose burdens grew no lighter in my
arms; the little ones smiled up despite my jealousy
however real; I might confess to not adoring
any one of them. Except, the humpty-dumpty

of our lives was but love's underpin, familiar,
daily as the skies that rose on them, the rhymes
I said to them, their first bo-peeping, recalling
nappies folded flat, warm towels I held,

plump bodies dripping wet, I close my eyes
again, rethinking spring, an evening
circles round me full of bathlight: imagine this
with powder sieving down on everything.

School Nurse's Journal

CELIA BROWN *Falmouth, Massachusetts*

Outside the school the kids swat about;
their swings jabber with them.
Just off the morning yellow bus,
being back to the books of no import,
hatted, coated, their bright-colored
wings see-sawing now on the sunlight.
Be prepared for anything
reads the motto on my office wall,
for scrapes, nosebleeds,
poison ivy, greenstick
fractures, chipped front teeth,
torn britches, wet clothes,
have something for those
who forget their lunch,

be watchful of bruises and sprains.
I check my cabinets again —
ice bags, bandages, sanitary pads,
peanut butter, and bread —
and draw up lists:
TD shots for tots at 10,
sports physicals at two,
dental hygiene, grade four,
conference with special ed.
Wheezing, chickenpox, name it,
get it. I don't mind the head lice
anymore, not since the mouse
last year, found fast asleep
and nesting in the upsweep
of Megan's hair, a cute farm critter,
just cut loose; Lord, so alive
and breathing. Let things drone,
this first school autumn day,
just a few larky flies coming in,
lured perhaps out of dung by
a whiff from the teachers' room.
As I listen for the first school bell
kids outdoors still buzz the yard,
their swings whirring with them:
higher and higher to pump at dreams,
airy as fifty snowflakes.

In the Solarium

CELIA BROWN *Falmouth, Massachusetts*

These winter plants remind me
of my old TB patients
in all their micro-climates
of green-stripe pajamas
and bright red hair.

How often they plucked
at the strings of my apron
as I bent over their beds:
half-well fellows
who thrived on blushes,
big sexy idle guys
intent on wooing the nurse.

I'd gather sputum cups anyway
and pass the PAS & INH.
But if Mother could have only seen
how they reached to me
and reached to me
as though I walked on sunlight
behind my X ray equipment
and thin flirtatious mask.

All Mother ever knew
were the letters I sent home
on Dettol-smelling paper;
letters that she shook out
in the fresh country air,
and burned
as soon as she had read them.

Mammography:
A Word with Grandma's Ghost

CELIA BROWN *Falmouth, Massachusetts*

They tell me I'm high risk too —
Grandma, you should see
their fancy machines!
My breast felt like a peach
between guillotines —

a painless execution perhaps
twenty years in advance.

I drove away for the weekend
to forget what the doctor thought.
Through all that wet August day,
like a rearview death in my mirror,
your shadow haunted memory
while frogs did a final road dance
on the way to Maine.

You would like it there, Grandma,
a sandy beach:
seadust between toes, and rooms —
salty crickets in your sleep;
and when you looked out
through the moulds of the morning,
the land raised like an Irish fist.

Body of Knowledge:
Remembering Diploma Schools, 1976

JEANNE BRYNER *Newton Falls, Ohio*

Where have I put the silver
bandage scissors they told me
never to lose, my student name tag,
the snowy candle I carried
for capping ceremony?

Where are the showers'
lathered girls, naked, laughing?
What's become of our housemother
bent over crossword puzzles
night after night?

Where is Louise Frye, who ran
out one autumn night screaming
I can't be a nurse.
Where is her father's Texaco shirt
and their sorry station wagon?

What were their names?
Those two girls who got ulcers
their junior year, and the one
with glasses who died from *leukemia*
that beautiful, beautiful word.

Gone are the thousand days
our professors stood patient
in ochre suits and wrote like cave painters,
something about pathways from the brain
to the heart, wanted us to remember.

Call and Response

JEANNE BRYNER *Newton Falls, Ohio*

Rebecca Anderson, nurse who died from head injuries
after trying to rescue people, Oklahoma City bombing

So this is the smell of trouble
the taste of blood. Me, buried
in rubble, trying to raise
my left hand, an answer
at last, to the teacher's question.

Over here, I want to say
to the siren's scream, the sound
of men telling me: *Stay back, get back.*

Your sewing machine's too far away,
Mom, and besides, there's no mending me now.
I grew tired of white ceilings, watching the game,
and never running a stop sign.

Courage blooms, a clap of thunder
in a dry forest, and maybe lightning's
the world's faint pulse, the point of life.
What have I done today
to make the world better? Miss Simpson
wrote on her blackboard, then turned around,
wheezing, facing us. In sixth grade,

it was call and response, me chewing M&Ms,
dreaming of marrying Donny Osmond.
But now, the medic's coffee breath above
me, his penlight checks my pupils.

My head's kicked in, a bruised
soccer ball half-filled with grits.

So this is the wind's roar,
the hungry wolf's yellow grin.

I want to say, *Yes, I forgot myself,*
forgot my hard hat to these firemen
who are lifting me, to the men shouting:
crazy woman, woman without a brain.

Standing There

JEANNE BRYNER *Newton Falls, Ohio*

Our history isn't an album of healers
dressed in snowy uniforms, white oxfords,
and halo caps. We do not saunter hallways
and giggle pink words.

This narrative is not about Merlin
or medicine men chanting blue power
over steamy rocks, nor is it a fist
against mahogany conference tables
or the kitten's whimper
in a rainstorm.

Our logbooks record moments
when pain was thunder, and we waited,
worked in a world of raw light
so bright its camera blinded.

Our story is a sea of brave faces
with grit teeth and shushed wings
and stalled hearts below glazed eyes.

Our story is how we did not shrivel,
though we were soaked, how we did not
freeze in the cold almost beyond bearing.

Our story is how we did not break
and run — no matter how close
the lightning gouged.

Breathless

JEANNE BRYNER *Newton Falls, Ohio*

Dear Trent, today I was remembering the clay faces of
parents pulling red wagons in Akron's pediatric hospital
and a three-year-old girl named Ashley with a brain
tumor the size of a melon, that pale train of four-year-
old boys pushing their IV poles like Sisyphus with his
rock day after day. Maybe you can't recall me, the
fumbling nursing student with hazel eyes, gripping her
pink spiral notebook, who mixed enzymes in your
applesauce. You drew me a picture that July, 1978. And it
was splendid too: your Mommy in her jeans and
gingham blouse, her boyfriend, Luke, on his Harley, the
one Mommy rode on weekends when she missed
visiting, and your beagle, Sam, wagging his tail by a
single blue flower. You handed it to me, pointing wildly
with your clubbed nails: *That's my dog, Sam. And that's
my house. That's where I live. Here, keep it.* It was
awfully cold that summer, and you didn't tell me what
to do with this painting you left behind. Please listen.
The oaks in my neighbor's pasture are awash today with
autumn's blush, and on some island, sandaled monks
are praying for war orphans, and me, I cradle almost
everything: my daughter's baby tooth, the smell of apple
fritters in my granny's kitchen, this faded manila paper
filled with Crayola marks. In the next room, Kenny G is
playing *Breathless* on his sax. Wherever you are Trent,
come sit with me in this horn's amazing shade. I know
now it's wrong to want more than this scrap of paper,
sinful to rescue angels.

Miscarriage:
The Nurse Speaks to the Baby

JEANNE BRYNER *Newton Falls, Ohio*

We are going back to the dirty
utility room, you floating
like a ballerina in a jar,
and me wondering how you found
an open space in the woods.
Little gardenia, you have split
your mother's heart.

To make a baby
for this world, women spin
a film of scarlet cobwebs
inside themselves, they ask
a blessing, to become a gourd,
a field where grain is grown.

You are the dancer
whose rhythm is not metrical,
and I name you abandoned flute.
You are the tiny globe
of two worlds, and I hold you,
a pale candle too wet to light.

You are the journey unwilling
to go forth, watercolors
touching the sky, spices
from a faraway land, daughter
of silk and air and dawn,
vine of warm ground
born to suffer loss.

What Nurses Do:
The Marriage of Suffering and Healing

JEANNE BRYNER *Newton Falls, Ohio*

Jane Ball, retired nursing supervisor

Compared to the day I had to sit with a mother
ask for her daughter's three-year-old kidneys
eyes, liver, and heart because a drunken
teenager had killed her brain
Compared to the afternoon I told a black man
his son was shot while jogging
Compared to the night I was paged to ER
to help sedate a seven-year-old girl
before they sewed her crotch
being here with this schoolteacher holding
her husband's hand, begging him to live
is better.

The rhythm of a heart repeats itself like vows
in a chapel full of light, but we are gathered
here because this man's heart choked after forty years
Medics shocked him, brought him back
Then, a cardiologist with his pacemaker, a respirator
We have stolen these minutes
but our bag has no more tricks, no more drugs
or gizmos, and now something as old as love
must be the pencil that helps the heart write
its good-byes across our screen.

I will never forget the wife's brown hair
and her tan corduroy blazer, how her face looked
when she asked for her husband's baptism
We couldn't reach a priest; it happens
They all looked at me, the nursing supervisor
I said I could

In the presence of this company
who gives this man to the next world?
The paper cup was blue, I asked a blessing
for the tap water and did it, water fell
soft as a kiss to his forehead.

And so I kept the devil far away
and let the wife cry into my shoulder
for a long time after
for a long time after.

The Radio

TERESA CAMPBELL *San Francisco, California*

It was 1960. I was in my senior year in a hospital nursing school when I was assigned to take care of Ken Taylor, a seventy-eight-year-old resident at a home for veterans who'd been brought to our hospital for evaluation. Ken had lost thirty pounds and had numerous complaints. The hospital often took in such "charity patients" if they could be used as teaching cases for the residents and interns. I was assigned to take care of Ken because the nurses considered him difficult; he yelled and always said he didn't want anything done for him. At morning report, it was obvious no one wanted anything to do with him either. Words like *cantankerous*, *surly*, and *disagreeable* were used to describe him.

When I entered the room in my blue and white striped uniform with my stiff starched apron and white hat, I saw a thin man with sparse gray hair lying in bed. His white hospital gown had the remnants of various meals splattered on the front of it. A wooden radio was playing on his bedside stand, and he yelled at me, "Get out!" I started to leave, then decided to stay and try talking with him.

"I'm here to give you a bath and your medication," I said. He grumbled something and turned his back. It was difficult to understand him; he didn't have any teeth and refused to wear his dentures. I fixed a basin of hot water, pulled back the sheet, and started bathing him. He glanced at me with amazement but didn't say a word.

He turned onto his back. I removed his gown, covered him with a bath blanket, and started to wash his arms with hot soapy water. Finally he said, "I guess I can't scare you away." I washed his dentures, too and, when I offered them, he slipped them into his mouth. At least I'd be able to understand him if he yelled at me. But in a clean bed with his hair combed, he looked like a different person. Once, he gave me a brief smile.

Every day for two months, I was assigned to care for Ken, and every day he talked a little bit more. He told me about the years he'd fought in World War II, how he'd watched his friends die, how much he'd loved his wife and child, and how they'd died too, in an automobile accident, and he told me how lonely he was living in a home for old veterans. On visitors' day, he sat alone. He would talk and we would listen to old-time music on his radio; he said it was his only possession and he wanted me to have it when he left. Student nurses couldn't accept gifts, I said, but I thanked him for his generous thought. I winked and said, "You don't have to give me gifts to win my love."

After a while, at morning report, nurses started to make comments like, "Ken isn't as grouchy as he used to be. He even said good morning to me." One nurse said, "He seems less irritable," and another nurse said how she didn't mind going into his room anymore. "He's not as cranky as he was when we first admitted him. I wonder what brought about the change?"

On my days off, different nurses were assigned to care for Ken. One red-haired nurse brought him a piece of cake she'd made. Another nurse brought bouquets of flowers from her garden and told him about the flowers as she put them in a vase.

After being away for a week's vacation, I returned to the unit. When I walked into Ken's room, he was gone. The head nurse saw me and called me out to her desk.

"Ken died in his sleep while you were away," she said. Then she pointed to the old wooden radio he and I had listened to so often. It sat on the counter amid the charts and lab reports, and attached to it was a note with my name on it. In his scribbled penmanship, Ken had written that I was to have the radio if anything should happen to him.

I didn't want to take the radio, but the head nurse insisted that it would be thrown away if I didn't. Now, forty years later, I still have the radio. When I play it, I remember Ken and the conversations we shared. He taught me that everybody has a story to tell, and everyone wants someone to listen. He taught me that listening to patients' stories is part of nursing. And I taught him that being able to tell that story is part of the healing process.

Slowly, Life Returned to Normal

excerpts from a memoir

SHULAMITH CANTOR
(*March 5, 1894 — December 25, 1979*)

I was the second of eleven children, seven girls and four boys. The boys attended Talmud Torah and the girls went to the Alliance Israelite Universalle. Upon graduation, scholarships would be given to the best students to provide four years' further study at the Teachers' Seminary in Paris. I was offered such a scholarship, but my parents did not permit me to leave home. My disappointment was great. Emotionally and socially, I was not ready to remain at home and wait for marriage. A compromise was found to permit me to continue my education at the American Seminary for Girls in Beirut, an American Missionary Institution. At the end of three years, one of my teachers, of whom I was very fond and in whom I confided my desire to study nursing, offered to give me a scholarship to the United States. Again my parents refused to let me accept. A second compromise permitted me to enter the American University Training School for Nurses in Beirut. I was admitted for the three-year course in the fall of 1915.

Nursing Training

Nursing training and education in those days was different from today. We donned our uniforms from the first day and went to the hospital ward with our teacher to learn bed-making. The emphasis was on the perfect corner and the stretched sheet. The daily schedule was from 7 A.M. to 7 P.M. with two hours off in between. Classes were held during our time off. We worked seven days a week with two half-days off. On our free day, we reported to work from 7 A.M. to 1 P.M. We were allowed to leave the campus but had to be back at 10 P.M. An overnight leave was granted upon a written request, but we had to report for duty as usual at 7 A.M. Night duty was from 7 P.M. to 7 A.M. The period for night duty was one month with one day off before reporting for day duty. All classes had to be attended during that time.

At that time, no evening shifts were known; neither were there night supervisors. Each head nurse of a pavilion was given a two-room apartment in that building. She was on call, if needed, at night. I remember, with great trepidation, wondering whether I should disturb her sleep when I was in a predicament about performing a certain treatment. The memory of the passing away of a patient (the first time I saw death) has never left me. It took months before I could regain my peace of mind.

During my first year, I was on night duty three times. On Sundays, every student was given half a day off, either in the morning or afternoon. When she had the morning off, she was expected to attend chapel at 11 A.M., irrespective of her faith. I made a vow to myself that upon completion of my studies I would go to Palestine and see that a school for nurses would be opened there, so that no Jewish girls should be forced to study nursing in a missionary school.

In the summer of 1918, while walking home during my afternoon off, I saw a station wagon on the side of which was printed a red shield and the name "Hadassah Medical Zionist Organization." It made news in Beirut. Everyone who noticed the car was curious to know what it was, to whom it belonged, and what the name inscribed on the side meant. After many questions and answers, I was told that a group of doctors and nurses called by the above name had arrived in Palestine. They were doing relief medical work in the hospital in Jerusalem and were going to open a school for training nurses in Palestine. Then and there, I decided that as soon as graduation was over, I would try to join Hadassah and help in the education of nurses.

World War I

During the First World War, all the able-bodied men in Asia Minor were drafted into the army and sent to Constantinople, the capital of Turkey, for the duration of the war. The country was left with elderly people, women, and children. Food was scarce and many people died from famine and disease. Families sent their children into the orphanages of Catholic convents or Protestant missions in order to save their lives. Lice was rampant, bringing with it typhus epidemics, and skin diseases were numerous. All the hospital wards were full, especially the children's department. Children were brought in with enlarged abdomens, all skin and bones. The first treatment was shaving their hair and feeding them. They weren't able to eat, although their eyes bulged at the sight of food. Very few survived, but the few saved slowly returned to normal. Many of them had no home to which to return.

My own father, unemployed and lacking the means to take care of the big family, had a nervous breakdown and was placed in a home outside of Beirut. The older children worked — my sister in an office and my brother in a bakery, receiving payment in bread for the family. Three of the younger ones were sent to a Day Home for their food. Mother cooked at home for some students so that the family could make the modest ends meet. It was one of the worst experiences of my life.

My First Contact with Zionism

As a full-fledged registered nurse, I returned home after graduation. My first employment was as a private duty nurse in the home of a Moslem family. Twenty-four-hour duty, seven days a week, was the rule until the patient recovered. During my second week, I was called home. The occasion was the arrival of my cousin D., who had returned from Constantinople after serving in the Turkish army, on an old French cargo vessel called *La-Gaule*. This cousin knew of my desire to go to Palestine and my wish to start a nursing school there. His first question was, "Well, when are you coming?" My answer was, I'm ready; I have my diploma now.

Come along on the boat, he told me. I accepted. I found a relief nurse, informed the doctor and family for whom I was working, and was released. The hardest part was convincing my mother to let me go. It was one thing to permit me to study nursing against their wish, but to leave home on my own was quite a different story.

It was the afternoon of a December day when I boarded the boat. My trunk, packed with all my books and belongings, was supposed to be my cousin's, and I was a visitor saying good-bye to him. The boat was old, rusty, and dark. There were no cabins, and the bottom hold was used as a dormitory for all the passengers. Camp beds with a blanket were the only equipment. As the time was nearing for the visitors to leave, a large bell was rung. I was taken to the hold and told to lie down and cover myself with a blanket. I remained there, for what seemed a very long time, when I felt the movement of the boat then heard singing and dancing on deck. I was the only one in the hold. My patience gave way, and I went up on the deck to see what was going on. The boys were singing and dancing, rejoicing at the thought of returning to their families the next morning. I was not the only spectator. The captain, officers, and another couple, Dr. and Mrs. Ticho, were also on deck.

Suddenly, someone grabbed my hand and asked in French, *Where did you come from, young lady?* I was puzzled and hardly able to talk. My cousin came to my rescue and explained that I came to bid him good-bye and did not hear the bell. The captain answered angrily, *I don't believe you. You will have to report to the police when we get to Jaffa.*

Dr. Ticho, standing by, was listening. I turned to him and explained that I was a trained nurse who'd just finished my course of study. I had heard about Hadassah, the American Jewish Organization, and wanted to join their work at the hospital in Jerusalem. Putting on a stern expression, the doctor said, "How do I know you are telling the truth?" In a very naïve way, I told him that I would show him my diploma. His wife felt sorry for me. *I shall talk to the captain if you promise not to shame me for helping you,* she said. I solemnly promised.

Nobody slept that night. The first light of sunrise appeared in the distance on Mt. Carmel, and still the singing and dancing continued.

In those days, boats could not enter the harbor because high rocks prevented smooth sailing. Strong Arab sailors screamed, *Yaala*, Oh God, as their large rowboats receded when the waves collapsed. This performance was repeated several times until the rowboats came near enough to reach the rope ladder thrown by our boat. Then one of the Arab sailors would take hold of the rope ladder and another would stand on the deck while the passengers were thrown into the rowboat into the arms of a third sailor. It took about an hour and a half from the boat to the harbor, but it seemed like days of uncertainty between life and death.

When I landed in Jaffa, there were no formalities to go through — no passport control, no customs, no health regulations. A porter was engaged to carry our luggage to a waiting car, and we drove through the city of Jaffa to my aunt's house in Tel Aviv. Her family was surprised to see the son-in-law returning home unannounced, followed by an unexpected guest. I explained that I had come to join Hadassah and work in one of their hospitals.

The next morning, taking my diploma, I went to see Dr. L., the director of the hospital in Tel Aviv, only to be told that they didn't need any nurses — Hadassah brought their own from America. My disappointment was great, almost to the point of tears. The doctor didn't even look at my diploma. I walked through the streets for almost an hour before returning to my aunt's house. A cousin tried to comfort me and suggested that I might apply to a French medical officer she knew. She'd heard that he was looking for a nurse to help him in his private surgical clinic.

I went to Jaffa, and the doctor engaged me at once; I started work the next day. A few days later, as we were working in the operating room, two officers were announced. They belonged to the Hadassah Medical Unit and, in between two operations, they asked the doctor how it was that he had a lay nurse instead of one of the nuns from the hospital. He told them that I was Jewish, a graduate nurse of the American University in Beirut, and he expressed his satisfaction at being able to engage me to assist him. Over cups of coffee, the officers asked me if I knew Hebrew, and why didn't I apply to Hadassah for work? Dr. R., who was the director of the Hadassah Medical Unit, told me that their unit was looking for a nurse with my qualifications. Hadassah enrolled a group of student nurses in Jerusalem, where a nursing school was being started. The students did their practice work under the supervision of American nurses in Yiddish, German, or Russian, but the students objected to being taught the theoretical subjects in any language other than Hebrew. The doctor offered me the post to teach nursing in Hebrew. I was so confused that I did not reply at once. I realized that my dream was coming true — I was to be the first instructor at the first school of nursing in Palestine.

Going Up to Jerusalem

In 1919, there were but two ways to reach Jerusalem — train or coach. Because of my big trunk, which could not be taken by coach, I had to go by train. A cab picked me up at 5 A.M. When I got to the station, all I saw were open carts used for carrying animals and other cargo. I asked the station master to direct me to the train for Jerusalem, and he pointed to the carts. I had my trunk put there and sat on top of it, riding there until the train stopped at Lydds, where I got onto the regular train. I recall the beautiful view of the Judean Hills and the comfort of the seats. The train reached the station in Jerusalem at 12:30 P.M., the identical station one sees in Jerusalem today. I took a cab to the Amdursky Hotel in the Old City outside the Jaffa Gate. After getting settled and having lunch, I went to report to the office of Dr. R., who gave me a hearty welcome. He called someone and told him to take me to the student nurses' home where a room was assigned to me.

*   *   *

Shulamith became the first Hebrew-speaking instructor at Hadassah's nursing school. She married Louis Cantor, leader of Hadassah's campaign to end malaria in Jerusalem. After Israel achieved independence, she was appointed director of nursing services for the Ministry of Health. Widowed in her thirties, she raised her four children alone.

*   *   *

The End of the British Mandate and the Beginning of the Nursing Division

The British Mandate was terminated on Friday, May 13, 1948. The high commissioner, Sir MacMichael, left Government House and the British flag was lowered. An hour later, the Yad Laumi, headed by David Ben Gurion, met in the Tel Aviv Museum and declared the birth of the state of Israel.

When the high commissioner left Government House, the troubles and shooting grew in intensity. Although a French flag as well as a Red Cross flag were raised on the roof of St. Joseph, the convent was bombarded. The Mother Superior offered us the use of a basement for a shelter, a tremendous, spacious place that the convent used for storing vegetables and other foods. The large rooms had meter-wide window sills all along the walls. We put mattresses on the sills and used them for the very sick patients who could not be removed when the bombing started. We also renovated two rooms and made a modern underground operating theater with all electrical conveniences and a special electric generator so that surgery could be done 24 hours a day. Post-operative cases were taken to rooms on the same floor until the patient was fully recovered. There were no utility rooms, so we opened a door leading to the garden where a temporary arrangement was made to empty bedpans into an outside water closet. The nurses and students worked very hard under these primitive conditions with no complaints; their satisfaction was the welfare and recovery of their patients.

During the siege of Jerusalem, food was rationed — 200 grams of bread per person, no milk or dairy products except powdered milk for the children, no electricity or kerosene, no fresh vegetables or fruit, only a small ration of dried peas or beans per family. People gathered branches of dead wood to boil water for tea. Dandelions were gathered and used in place of spinach. Water was brought in barrels on a truck and people of all classes queued with their pans and pails in order to receive their four gallons of water per person twice weekly. Blackouts were the order of the day and were enforced. People opened fences between their homes to avoid using the streets. It took a long time to reach one's destination because of the shooting. One would throw oneself to the ground to avoid the shrapnel.

On Shavuoth of that year, I went to visit my friend, Rabbanit Herzog. She received me gleefully and told me that she had a surprise treat for me. She came from the kitchen holding a plate with an orange and a tomato. I opened big eyes and wondered how she got them. She explained that her son, Haim, an officer in the army, was stationed at Latrun. He was given a few hours leave for the holiday and brought her some fresh fruits and vegetables. I looked at the orange and could not touch it. When she asked me the reason, I answered that I could not eat it without sharing it with my children. She understood, and I took it home. The children were happy to have such a treat, but we decided together to enjoy looking at it for a day or two and eat it later with gusto.

The fighting in the Old City continued. Every day toward evening I heard the boys singing while going to reinforce the soldiers in the Old City. When they returned after midnight, they were very quiet, because they'd left many of their comrades wounded or dead.

The streets of Jerusalem were deserted all the time. The food shops were empty except for some mustard or spices which nobody bought. The noise of the shooting and bombing was constant. When a two-day armistice was imposed on both sides in order to clear the dead and the wounded, suddenly the streets were full of people, babies, and carriages. After the armistice, fighting resumed. One of our best nurse midwives was killed by a stray bullet when she was reporting for duty.

The worst day of the siege was a Friday, the last day of the fighting. The shooting was continuous the entire morning. It took me two and a half hours to reach St. Joseph convent, walking along the walls and stretching out on the ground many times to avoid shrapnel. The streets were full of bloodstains.

People looked different, so much so as not to be recognizable. Most of them lost weight and looked very pale. Our out-patient department, which was always very crowded, was quieter. Fewer patients came for medical care. But slowly, life returned to normal. The roads were opened and communication with the rest of the country was becoming normal. Mail started to reach Jerusalem. Food packages were sent by friends from Tel Aviv and Haifa. Tinned fruit, vegetables, jam, sugar, rice, and many other goodies were enjoyed after the famine diet during the siege.

I'd received a letter from Dr. Nissan, the newly appointed director general of the Ministry of Health of the State of Israel, asking me to come to Tel Aviv to organize the Division of Nurses. My reply was that my place was in Jerusalem as long as the siege was on, and I would only be able to leave when quiet was restored. It was agreed that I should be on loan from Hadassah for a year to organize the Division of Nursing. Early in August, I reported to Dr. Nissan at Sarona, a suburb of Tel Aviv. When I asked him for some suggestions, he said, "You know what is needed. Draw up a plan and start!"

* * *

In 1955, at the age of sixty, I insisted upon retiring from the Ministry of Health, but remained two months to break in the new director of the Nursing Division. During the last month, while introducing her to the various institutions in the country, I was banqueted everywhere and presented with gifts. The Ministry of Health had arranged a parting evening at the Asaf Harofe Hospital in Sarafend. All the directors of the hospitals and schools of nursing in Israel were invited. My Nursing Division staff prepared a sketch, "This Is Your Life," in which they successfully depicted the young stow-away nurse sailing to Palestine to teach nursing. They covered the many stages of my professional life to the time of my retirement as the first director of the Nursing Division of the Ministry of Health of the State of Israel. As usual at such parties, many speeches were made with compliments and appreciation of all the pioneering work I had done.

I was very touched and could not control my tears. All I could say was *Thank you.*

Good-bye

ALICE CAPSHAW *Berkeley, California*

I stroked your arm slowly from shoulder to wrist.
I didn't have to.

I cupped your cheeks in my hands and combed your hair
with the part just the way you liked it.
I didn't have to.

I shined a flashlight into your mouth to see what I could see.
I'm not sure why.

Then I tied the name tag on your big toe,
wrapped your head in the paper sling,
rolled you into the flimsy plastic shroud,
folding each end carefully.
This I had to do.

What Nurses Do Best

MARLENE CESAR *Miramar, Florida*

I'm at the nursing station concentrating on what nurses do best
    today — paper work! — when suddenly,
the heavy door separating the Psych ward from the rest of the
    world opens
and the charge nurse stands up and mourns, "Another
    admission! More work, more work,

and not enough help!" Then, reality strikes. A *real* patient, a
    human being to be transformed
by this system, the same system that created this nursing
    shortage that has left us with work,
more work for those who dare stay and try to look their best
    after a 16-hour shift.

Oh, the patient! "Yes. He is mine."
I have to develop a certain short-term relationship with him.
    I start the Pysch admission history,
putting together the puzzle of his life — jobless, homeless, no
    money,

no family support. To garnish the paperwork (very important for
    this bureaucratic system)
my interrogation continues, my detailed history soon to appear
    in the care plan
as "other medical conditions not addressed in this
    hospitalization." Then comes my assessment —

a quick one. (Remember, he is a Psych patient. I have to
    concentrate on his mind today.)
Mind, he might not have one anymore when he starts asking for
    his PRN. Anyway, our relationship
continues. I inquire about his inner feelings, his emotions, his
    suicidal ideations.

Then, only then, will I grant him permission to smoke one, two,
    three cigarettes,
killing his lungs. Next comes the endorsement of the paper
    work. What? Is he voluntary?
Involuntary? Was he "Baker-acted?" (All this jargon to satisfy
    the system, the same one

that provides him drugs in the streets, that takes him in and
    offers sporadic treatment
with those same drugs.) And the same diagnosis: schizophrenia,
    major depression (recurrent and
severe with psychotic features). More work, more work for
    nurses who are alone,

still dreaming of Florence Nightingale and all the grand
    theorists, dreaming
of what it *used* to be: Therapeutic communication. Nurse-client
    relationship. So close to my patient.
And yet so far.

In the OR

ROBIN CHARD *Hollywood, Florida*

We live
here behind our masks, here, being ourselves.
Behind our masks is who we are:
your caregivers, your protectors, your guardians.
Look beneath the mask, look beyond these layers of protection.
You will see us: our essence, our nature, our love.

The Color of Blood

VICTORIA MAY COLLETT *Port Washington, New York*

He's standing two feet across from me and his hand is trembling, albeit only slightly. Barely enough for me to notice. Nevertheless, I know his mind is careening over the precipice. While everybody else in the OR thinks he's close to a god incarnate, I don't. I know him.

I'm as familiar with this man as I am with the varied shades of blood — from brilliant cadmium to stinking, sulfuric sepia.

"Get the damn pump sucker in here, Liz!" is what he says to me, as calm as you please, like he's quietly demanding more ice in his piña colada while he languishes on a pale, striped deckchair down there in sunny, oblivious Ocho Rios.

The words haven't finished coming out of his mouth before I whip the pump sucker right into that open chest, sucking up enough blood to satisfy a dehydrated vampire. Blood is all over my latex hands and blue paper arms, congealing as it hits any surface outside its own home body. My gloves feel tacky and thick blood glues the end of the pump sucker to my stuck-together fingers. So what if I struggle to hold the thing in the patient's chest? When this particular surgeon demands something, he wants it yesterday and nothing, not blood or tissue — certainly not sticky fingers — gets in his way. The dying heart, spewing cups of blood with every lessening beat, is his only concern — along with how the SEC could investigate ECNC, that new stock he's invested heavily in.

When you're *the* favorite scrub nurse, you get to have this kind of relationship with a surgeon. It bonds you in a way that makes words unnecessary. When he tells you that the patient's chances of survival with this particular man-induced heart anomaly (an atrioventricular groove tear) are ninety-five percent, you know he truly means that one hundred percent of those patients fall into the fatal five percent category. Needless to say, words aren't really necessary.

You'd hate like hell to have to go home with him, because as soon as the case is over, you're not half as intelligent as you are while he's cutting into the patient's heart, deftly sliding cannulae into the aorta and vena cava. It's someone else who promptly hands him the suture that most times saves the case. It's someone else who instantly deciphers his spasmodic hand gestures into what he really wants. It's someone else who, at the beginning of surgery, drapes his patient and sets up his pump lines — exactly the way he likes it. While he struggles with his higher issues, he expects what he knows you know — and God forbid you don't. You know one thing — the patient's aorta is dissecting — shredding — right in front of his very eyes and blood is bubbling, obscuring his vision, gushing like the fountain of Merlot he talks about in the foyer of the Palm, his favorite restaurant.

He doesn't want you as his mistress, and you'd decline that offer anyway because you've caught a glimpse of him naked in the men's locker room. Despite his thousand-watt smile, his Armani suits, and his self-inflated ego, he also has flabby arms and a hairy butt, so you'd pass him up. It happens this way: the hospital pays you thirty-something dollars an hour and that covers your rent and your charge card bills. But it's the short-lived thrill of the emergency that keeps you with him at the field — the equality he bestows upon you for fleeting seconds as the blood that binds you pumps out of the body and tumbles over the sides of the operating table and onto the floor.

Like now!

"Put pledgets on the damn sutures, Elizabeth. And make 'em big enough to cover damn Shea Stadium. I got a damn problem here." He uses profanity only when he's in deep trouble, in this case, deep blood. By now, my favorite white sneakers (canvas Keds with little hearts embroidered on the sides, covered with blue paper OR booties), are a lost cause. I'll have to ditch them if I can't wash out the blood in the basement washing machine in the apartment complex where I live in a studio with a Siamese cat called Bundlebranch and five hundred monoprints from when I wanted to get right out of this nursing business and become an acclaimed artist.

So it didn't work out, and now I'm stuck here watching this patient's heart bleed out as surely as John Travolta blew away some poor guy in *Pulp Fiction*, spreading blood, egg yokes, and other debatable substances to the four winds.

"Damn it, the heart is falling apart." *Damn, damn, damn* and worse, is all the surgeon keeps saying, more to himself than to anyone else. "Get the Crazy Glue in here. Get somedamnthing. Quick."

After a nanosecond I know where this is going.

"This patient is no good. No good. Someone tell the nursing supervisor to get in touch with the relatives. Tell them the patient is having a small setback in the OR," he hisses to the anesthesiologist, who is already reaching for the phone on the wall.

"Always give them hope," is what he says in a whisper no one but me can hear. As he says this, I know the patient is as good as dead because one hundred percent of that fatal five percent has just kicked in. My surgeon's hand is visibly trembling as he plunges the cannula into a section of intact aorta. He jams the venous cannula into the superior vena cava, hurriedly connects the cannulae to the pump lines and croaks aloud for perfusion — *On Bypass*.

He may say, *On Bypass*, but that doesn't mean the patient is going to comply. Right now, there is no blood flowing through the clear plastic tubing. Bypass is only when blood *is* bypassing the heart via the plastic lines to the cardiopulmonary pump. Well, this man's blood is bypassing everything via the floor. Anesthesia — a wiry, wild-haired PhD in physics before he got into medical school, a guy who wants to believe in the afterlife — manually squeezes bags of scarlet packed cells through an IV into a widebore neck line. Blood goes in the patient's neck and comes out his chest onto me standing where the first assistant, the cardiac fellow, usually stands. I think the cardiac fellow is still out at the scrub sink, scouring every goddamn particle of humanity off his skinny hands.

During these perilous, emergent times of bodily spills, I always gaze quickly around the room to see if I can spot any souls departing, rising up, leaving the body to the mere mortal hands of a cardiac surgeon who sometimes thinks he's God. A couple of times in emergencies like this one, I have felt a strange presence. But when all hell is breaking loose and the surgeon is either dead calm or freaking out, barking orders, blubbering incoherently to himself, infusing his sentences with a variety of swear words, and I'm jamming sutures into his trembling hand, it's hard to appreciate the metaphysical side of life.

The here and now is what I'm fixated on.

It's that holier-than-thou relationship we've got going. On

cases such as this, I might as well be married to the guy. I feel his every thought before he thinks it, and now his fear is pervading me like some shadowy sinister virus. I can even recognize the smell of his sweat above the pungent odor of the patient's darkening spilled blood. Sometimes, during emergencies, he whispers to me, *It's a brown boxer case, Lizzie*.

It's still my fault however, when he stabs himself with a needle or cauterizes his own flesh through his glove. It's me who gets to hear him bad-mouth the nursing staff for all having zero IQs while he elevates the resident to demigod because she/he took a good vein from the patient's leg (despite a leg incision closure that looks like an experiment in surgical horror). It's my fault when his loupes fog up and his headlight sucks and the suction doesn't suck and he'd like a piece of broken bottle to cut the suture because the damn scissors don't cut, thank you very much. It's my fault when the first assistant cuts a suture that immediately unravels an entire distal anastomosis on the artery at the back of the heart during an Off Pump Coronary Artery Bypass using a new suboptimal retractor that slides instead of immobilizing the beating surgical site. It's my fault when he traumatizes the atrial wall with a plastic suction tip, since I put the suction in his hand.

His constant complaints notwithstanding, it's only me he wants to scrub for all his cases because he does not want to have to ask the poorly-trained scrub nurses for instruments when he's going on bypass and giving stock market tips. He wants *me* because he puts out his hand and the instrument or suture is slapped into it within the heartbeat it takes him to fold his fingers around said object. He hates to interrupt himself to ask for a purse string or a pull-up or scissors or a clamp or a blade or an awl or a cannula. He only gives me the briefest accusatory eye contact if someone else is pissing him off; that's my fault too. I say, who needs eye contact when you are bound by blood that's not yours nor his — bonds stronger than some little strip of gold around the ring finger of your left hand.

And six hours later, when the patient's heart is stitched back together with enough felt to start a hat factory and Crazy-Glued for extra holding power, we stagger out of that OR like we've just gone through a lifetime together. He doesn't bother to thank me, because he believes that's my job anyway. So there. The dictating phones beckon him even before he speaks to the relatives and he *feels like hell* he says, *but believe me, Liz, I'm not the one who is lying on that table. Hell is fine.*

All I feel like is, I just washed out his boxer shorts in the washing machine downstairs in the apartment complex where I live with a Siamese and a computer that's going to get me so far away from this nursing business, I won't be able to remember the color of blood.

Career Day

CORTNEY DAVIS *Redding, Connecticut*

She stood, starched white.
Her silver scissors glistened,
the fluted jewel of a nursing pin
nestled against her breast.
I was seventeen — restless
with leftover passion, watching
the shirt move over the back of the boy
three seats forward. She hushed us,
a hiss of cotton against silk,
then she said *pain* and *shot*
and there, in that bright arena,
a crescendo of moans
rose like sweet violins. I enrolled.

I learned how cells collide
then meld and peel into spheres,
multisided like soccer balls
or Rubik's Cubes gone wrong.
I stabbed oranges until my hands
ran with juice; then patients
until my hands rang with grace.
I learned the quick save:
airway entered upside down
and turned into breath. I learned

to kiss death, my lips seeking
those slack mouths, while the boy
waited, flicking his bright cigarette,
the burning eye that led me, my shift over,
to his embrace. Even there,
I longed for the silent corridors
where patients slept in stupor
thick as grief. Where the night nurse

moved in my favorite dance —
pianissimo, pale through hospital halls.

The Swan by the Mall

CORTNEY DAVIS *Redding, Connecticut*

The swan's white bulk, crumbled like a corrugated box,
rolls from side to side with the rush
of passing cars, its feathers angled up like a broken fan.
I drive by, and as I do I see an angel rise from the swan's body,
hover briefly, then turn to look at me
as it opens its wings and circles like a helicopter.
When an angel rose from Joe Costanzo the same joy
came over me. Joe had just exhaled that long
whoosh, the breath that empties the lungs even before
the heart's last thump. As Joe's pulse leapt into the room,
I saw his pupils dim, like candles damped
with two moist fingers. It was a busy Wednesday,
nurses rushing about. Then the angel,
unfolding itself and blinking.
The rest of the shift, white gauze was tender
under my fingertips, and blood had the fragrance of peonies.
Other nurses nodded, each recalling her stories:
One angel spoke. Another stole a ring and hid it
in her pocket.
                    The swan disappears,
and I pull into the parking lot. Who wouldn't hurry
to the bedside of the dying, just to see the angel again as it goes,
drawing itself from death's shrunken belly into the room?

Every Day, the Pregnant Teenagers

CORTNEY DAVIS *Redding, Connecticut*

assemble at my desk, backpacks
jingling, beepers on their belts like hand grenades,
and inside, their babies
swirl like multi-colored pinwheels in a hurricane.

The girls raise too-big smocks, show me
the stretched-tight skin
from under which a foot or hand thumps,
knocks, makes the belly wobble.

A girl strokes her invisible child,
recites all possible names, as if a name
might carry laundry down the street or fix
a Chevrolet. I measure months

with a paper tape, maneuver the cold stethoscope
that lifts a fetal heart-*swoosh* into air.
Then, shirts billowing like parachutes,
the girls fly to Filene's where infant shoes,

on sale, have neon strobes and satin bows — *oh*,
Renee, Shalika, Blanca, Marie,
the places you'll go, the places you'll go!

Water Story

CORTNEY DAVIS *Redding, Connecticut*

I love the living sound of my plant when I water it,
the hiss and suck of agua
pulled through the soil by gravity,
the sweat that appears on the clay pot,
the unwrinkling of the leaves.
I had a patient once, pregnant mother
morning sick and evening sick, who arrived
hauling her children, carrying her bucket.
We slipped a needle in her vein,
dripped saline into her body's dry core
and, right before me, the woman
plumped up. My ivy overflows —
a thread of water and fertilizer returns to earth
through the sink mouth. I am happy
that all life is circular. Seven months later,
the woman's chubby boy popped out, head first.
Blood and water flooded the catch basin, spilled over.
I carry this story on my white shoes.

How I'm Able to Love

CORTNEY DAVIS *Redding, Connecticut*

I'm stunned by death's absence,
by the flesh that remains, changed and yet hardly so.
I try to pretend the body's a pod or insect shell,
but attending the body after death

I see the body with all its attributions
for the first time, totally honest —
a time to satisfy that final curiosity,
the long gaze that reveals a life compressed, unalterable.

Beyond the window, rain falls. Streets below
shine like an untied black ribbon.
When my mother died, I was the one
part nurse, part daughter. I caught her last heartbeat

with my fingertips, knowing that the lungs
fail a few beats after, then breath empties them.
From long experience, I stood at the moment
just before and stroked her hair

as life moved through her as it always does —
pulling itself up through the ankles
through the bruised aorta
taking the heartbeat along, gathering the last

lungful of air and leaving nothing, all this
up through the jaw and, at the moment life breaks free,
out the open eyes. The hands respond,
as if the body wasn't robbed, but had been clinging and let go.

I don't believe in death.
Even when the body mottles, even
in its closed casket, I see the body I have touched,
staring at it as I work. Only my fingers

retain the memory
of my memory. This compression is good:
it makes room for all the dead I know and don't know —
the familiar dead and the dead yet to be born.

The Other Side of Illness

CORTNEY DAVIS *Redding, Connecticut*

I heard a nurse say *Your operation is over.* I had been a long time waking. As I swam back toward the sounds of the recovery room, I was aware of hands touching my arms and adjusting what seemed to be an endless number of new appendages — tubes and wires that snaked from my body like bare branches on a winter tree. Ah, I thought. This one must be a nurse, the owner of the voice that's saying *good-bye, good luck.* Then there was a lurch and a floating sensation as my gurney was whisked away.

When all motion stopped, I vaguely realized I was in my room. A centipede with a hundred hands lifted me from the stretcher to the cold bed. More hands rolled me from side to side, then a woman who smelled like soap enfolded me in a warm blanket, and I disappeared.

I hadn't been a patient for many years. Just days ago, I had been the strong nurse on the other side of illness. When I found myself lying in the Emergency Room, subjected to all those odious procedures to which I once glibly sent my patients, I was reminded of how thin the line is between health and sickness. How easy it is to feel *good.* How quickly we can give that up and fall helplessly into disability's deep crevice.

For the next several days, I wondered if I would live or die, then chided myself for such dramatics. I struggled to make sense of my symptoms, repeating to myself that the weird nightmares were due to the central nervous system effects of the antiemetics, that the nasogastric tube was indescribably uncomfortable because it was irritating my nasopharynx, and that the unremitting nausea was a hangover from the anesthesia. Whenever I floated to consciousness, I took inventory of my body, as patients have told me they've done: *Yes, my heart is beating. Yes, I feel pain, so I must be alive.*

I could rationalize my symptoms, but clinical mastery didn't calm my fears. All the while, the nurses came and went from my bedside, changing medications, soothing me, holding my hand when there was nothing else they could do. For the first time, I realized the importance — the impact — of this kind of consistent, nonjudgmental caring. While doctors visited once daily and gave their brief pronouncements, nurses were ever present, comforting me and standing vigil over the workings of my body — the rise and fall of oxygen, measured by the clip on my index finger; the fluctuation of blood pressure and the ooze of fluid from my incision; the rewrapping of bulky antiembolic pads that whooshed and squeezed my legs all day and night. That reassuring rhythm contrasted with the growing necessity I felt to hold on to what was *normal* — if one could recall what it was like to be a whole person, I reasoned, one could set a course to recapture that feeling. I also wondered if I was in this situation because I needed to discover what it was *really* like to be a patient. Perhaps I had grown too complacent after twenty-seven years in practice, and had failed to be as alert as I should have been. I decided that someone had found me out, and sent me here for repair.

So I paid attention to what I saw and thought about in the dark. Sometimes I'd wake and see a nurse, like a dream vision or a cool drink offered in the midst of a suffocating desert, standing over me to adjust the equipment that kept my body in equilibrium. Then I understood what *my* presence as a caregiver meant to the patients I've tended.

I also gained a new appreciation of how suffering alters time. The clock on the wall glowed in the dim light. Whenever I looked, only minutes had passed, as if fear grasped the slender hands and held them back, magnifying every bodily sensation and dragging out every pain as if it were taffy, sickly sweet and stretched to the breaking point. As hours inched by, I realized how mortal and common I was — just one patient on a floor filled to capacity. Nevertheless, I reminded myself, we patients each have our own unique tale, our individual suffering.

Little by little I recovered, and as I did, the nurses' routines changed. They lingered to talk. They fussed about my flowers, snipping off withered blooms and tipping cupfuls of water into the vases. They made sure I had everything I needed: my comb, my magazine, the call bell pinned to my johnny coat. They entered my room less often, and whole nights went by without their disturbances.

A day before my discharge, they moved away from me completely, setting me free like a mother lets go of her child. This progressive separation was, I realized, a dance as well rehearsed as a complicated madrigal. In the beginning, the nurses' actions intertwined with mine, close and magical. As I needed less, they moved away in ever widening circles, until suddenly I found myself dancing on my own.

My brief illness allowed me to look at my nursing role from another vantage. All along, I had known how we caregivers move in and out of a patient's grief or happiness, changing our expressions, lowering our voices, going from one room that is blessed to another that has gone cold as January. Like others, I've collected the stories — patients blasted with disease who should have died, but didn't. Healthy patients who died anyway, perhaps not of a broken body, but of a shattered soul. Now, more than ever, I understood how someone could will themselves to die, or how, to a point, patients might will themselves to live.

I also learned how caregivers' and patients' experiences intertwine. For that terrible, suspended time of illness, patients sink into our care wholly and confidently. They let us carry them. They come to know us — not the details of our lives, but the intent of our souls — as intimately as we come to know the secrets of their flesh.

Today when I stand at a patient's bedside, I see my actions through their eyes, and the sense that my illness served as a warning lingers. *Pay attention nurse!* it says. *What you do and who you are when you care for a patient is significant. Your presence etches a chapter into the story of that patient's life that can never be erased.*

Marisol

THEODORE DEPPE *County Donegal, Ireland*

When I quit my nursing job
   to write in Ireland
      I stepped out into summer stars

and clicked my heels in the air.
   Security cameras
caught my leap

      and the supervisor
   froze the frame all night
so day shift could see
that look of pure joy.

   Strange now to think
      Marisol had just been readmitted.

   Did Dante feel guilty
as he left the inferno? — all those voices calling
      remember us to the living —

I can be watching the island children
   run down the pier after a field trip
      to the mainland,

      or a hooded crow
might drop a mollusk on the rocks
      to crack its shell, and —

Beautiful Marisol.
   Her pale, dirty face framed
      by matted black hair.

Some keenness behind those dark eyes
            as if she'd been raised
    by wolves.

    Marisol, who'd stabbed her foster father
with a pencil, her fourth failed placement,

        Marisol, who'd first
come to our children's unit
    when she was five — something broken

        behind those eyes, and fierce —
    she'd bit off the head of a parakeet.

At the seawall, the island children call
    to the spring tide to swell up
        and pelt them
            with rocks and spray.

    They shriek,
            cover their heads and run,
    then return laughing to the slipway
        and taunt the sea again.

            And the children
    in the hospital courtyard?
    Those who will call out to anyone

            beyond the high, link fence?
Want to or not, I see them:

        Marisol walks on low stilts
    through the locked garden
        and won't look at her birthmother

    who's finally come to visit.
She plants one leg down and
        swings her hip into

                   the next step, striding
through the blaze
    of sunflowers:

        her mother and that nurse
        can go to hell
    while this dance is played out,

                back straight, head high,
        everyone calling.

Counting the Children

THEODORE DEPPE *County Donegal, Ireland*

Five kids round up fiddler crabs into blue plastic-bucket
    dungeons.
Downbeach, two girls tease gulls with sandwich crusts.

Mary's in the water, showing Joel how to float on his back.
Joel, who was discharged last week and then walked two miles

back to the hospital to beg for his old room.
Mary says, sometimes you have to let the water hold you.

Above us gulls bicker, the sky's greedy with bright wings and
    yellow eyes.
Mary cups one hand beneath his head, supports his spine, lets go,

and when he starts to sink catches him, coaxes him to trust the
    ocean.
Joel, who told us his sister will die if he talks too much.

Thousands crowd the hot sands. Everything's so quiet.
Ears beneath the water, there's nothing but water's nothing
    sound.

What Thomas Wanted

THEODORE DEPPE *County Donegal, Ireland*

From the air, our meadow must have seemed the one safe place
to land. Thunderclouds glowered as the hot-air balloon
slid silently to meet its shadow — or did the hospital field
rise to meet the newlyweds waving from their basket? Children
came running, the balloon master bowed to them, the kids
    wanted
to push up close and see "the Mommy"

though I doubt this bride was a mother —
she hardly knew what to say, placed
by chance before this clamor of kids who wanted
to touch her silk dress. No escape in the balloon,
its brilliant colors folded behind her. Finally, she let the children
stroke her smooth sleeves, which wasn't enough: Thomas
    wanted to feel

her floral headpiece, wanted a hug. On the windy field,
holding Thomas in her arms, the bride swayed like a frightened
    mother.
Last Sunday in group therapy I asked the children
"who would you like to meet if you could travel anyplace?"
Thomas wanted to see his mother. He gave the heart-shaped
    balloon
he'd painted in art group to his foster mom, then wanted

it back when she was leaving. It was his first gift, she wanted
to keep it, he bit her wrist. Our freshly mown field
must have glided like safe haven toward the balloon.
The storm broke, the "Daddy and Mommy"
sheltered with us in the hospital. What must this place
have seemed to them? One of the kids

screamed in the quiet room. Some of the children
wanted her to hold them. The bride wanted

coffee, a cigarette, and a peaceful place
to smoke. Outside, under the eaves, she stared at the field
where a girl only hours a wife had landed and found herself a
    mother.
I tried to imagine the scene at the church as the balloon

lifted off, the groom proclaiming over champagne "let this
    balloon
take us wherever the wind blows." That night, when I tucked the
    kids
in bed, Thomas asked about his jailed mother,
wanted reassurance Dad wasn't outside, but he also wanted
to say he'd been the first to see the balloon glide down toward
    our field.
Thomas, who may prove unplaceable,

wanted the balloon to come back tomorrow, take the kids on a
    field trip
someplace great. He said the balloon was "like a beach ball as big
    as a beach."
I laughed, so he kept on: "the balloon was like a circus without
    noise."

Children's Unit Blues

THEODORE DEPPE *County Donegal, Ireland*

It ends with Louis Armstrong banned from the children's ward.
The Armstrong tape I left behind banned from the children's
    ward.
The newest memo protects our kids from "It's a Wonderful
    World."

It begins with Hector Baptiste, nine-year old from New
    Orleans,

The music wars begin with Hector, black kid from New
    Orleans,
Quickmarched to time-out when his taunts get too obscene.

He says his therapist hates him, he swears that I'm a queer.
He promises he'll kill us both if it takes a hundred years.
Then he's calling for his mother, the bitch who dumped him
    here.

The supervisor wants Vistaril to silence Hector's shouts.
Wants Vistaril to drug him up, she's sick of all the shouts.
I put on Coltrane's "Alabama," see if that'll drown him out.

At first it's just more noise, the horn and Hector's screech,
Tenor sax is clashing with the boy's shrill screech,
Then a violent sort of beauty wobbles just out of reach.

A moment comes when screams & sax both rise up together.
A moment when the shouts & horn both lament together.
Then a whole grief world glides above this corridor.

John Coltrane's got it all down, hopeless and shining.
Somehow Coltrane's got it down, all the pain one dark shining.
Trane's talking soft, Hector shuts up, listening.

Hector's in the time-out room pretending he's got a horn,
Leaning on the padded walls he's wailing on a phantom horn,
He's playing out each rotten year he's known since he was born.

Surprised to see him settle down, I put on a tape of Armstrong.
Coltrane's done, try one more tape, sweet rasps of Louis
    Armstrong.
What else can I give him? His stay here won't be long.

Oh, let the unit director have her senseless final word.
She thinks she's going to help by censoring songs and words.
Hector, blues come like a thief, hold fast to what you heard.

One on One with Dylan Thomas

THEODORE DEPPE *County Donegal, Ireland*

I'm taking my break outside the detox unit,
          watching a junkie shoot baskets in the parking lot,
admiring the lazy arc and swish of her fifteen-footers,

          when a scrap of last night's dream returns:

I'm one on one with Dylan Thomas,
          who drops his shoulder
          and drives baseline, reversing his lay-up so the ball
spins on the rim and drops in.

He's short and slow and
          impossible to guard:
                    feint to the right, three quick steps to the basket
                              before he shovel flips
          the ball around me.

Maybe it's time to find another job.
Maybe the last time I made a difference here
     is months past, before this place began to
          traffic in quick cures.

Years ago, Coach Froligher ordered me to quit
          our high school production of Dylan's *Under Milk Wood.*
          Coach,
          quietly intense, got what he wanted
                    by speaking so softly his players leaned

towards him, off balance, to hear.
          He wanted me to think
                    only of the next game,
                              wanted everything to ride on it.

Sometimes I tell the story of why I quit the team
        as though it began
                my present life,
Dylan's voice echoing in mine as I strode off court,
        though I imagine
                my last words to Coach were
                        high-pitched
                and graceless, abject stubbornness pressed to decide.

The junkie — a woman named Noni I've only talked with once,
        whose habits and boyfriend force her to turn tricks —
                has asked an orderly for a light.
I like the way the ball's release and cigarette's removal from her
    lips
        are one motion, her deft handling of
                awkward transitions, how she exhales and
rebounds an errant shot, fires again,
                two hand jumper, this one
        kissing
                the rim, swirling through before the long drag's
                        prompt reward.

What could I say
        that would help her walk out
                next time she's ordered to sell herself
        for a nickel bag?

"Begin at the beginning" Dylan intones,
        the Caedmon recording I bought
bringing back the play's smokelit opening night,
                a few months before his death.

Words can't save us
        though I walked off court, however tongue-tied,
                intoxicated
                        by the slap and surge of slow vowels.
This must be the boyfriend,
                        long sleeved on a sweltering day,
        come to take Noni on pass.

          Let him tell Noni
   one too many times
      "you'll never be anything
      but a strung-out whore."

Let him break
   her nose again, if that's what it takes.

Too long I've fought against
   becoming one thing or the other:

         all right damnit, force us to choose.

Autopsy No. 24722

SANDRA BISHOP EBNER *Litchfield, Connecticut*

Dead February 4th. He was sixty-five. That's young, isn't it?
Patient with a ten-year history
of intermittent claudication, documented
inferior wall myocardial infarction.
A photograph shows him young. So handsome.
He would pour black molasses on his plate,
soak it up with bread, joke about
what he might run out of first, molasses
or bread; if molasses, add molasses, if bread, bread.
No way to end, he'd grin.
The right coronary artery almost
completely occluded one centimeter from its origin.
Yesterday morning, snow until midnight. Can each flake
be different? Clumps fall from pines — their branches
laden, lift again to tree shape.
The LAD 90% stenosed two centimeters from the bifurcation.
The circumflex contains numerous plaques.
The cat eyes me from outside the window.
What does its longing feel like?
What will my children remember of me?
How thin the skin that covers my veins.
Catheterization revealed almost complete
occlusion of right coronary.
My mother walks from the altar.
Host dissolving on her tongue, she drops to her knees,
a prayer position, heavy head lowered to her arms,
my father surrounded by flowers.
Contrast material fills the vein
in a retrograde manner
from the left coronary. Little filling seen
distal to anastomosis.
Where is the space between children
and their grief?
How else do the dead resurrect themselves?

Myocardial fibrosis — extensive.
Mother's sobbing is the finest offering,
better than Hail Marys, better than the whole Rosary —
a Novena — her no-words shaking. The lost husband
will not know the holiness of this sorrow.
I am afraid to touch her
before I kneel down to hold her.

The Shape of the Human Spine

SANDRA BISHOP EBNER *Litchfield, Connecticut*

Multiple Sclerosis: the breakdown of the myelin sheath that surrounds
and protects the brain and spinal cord.

The patient picks up
a wrench from the table
in her one-bedroom apartment,
asks me to tighten
the bolts on her wheelchair.
It moves when the brakes are on.
Her face red — *I need to go into*
a nursing home — conjunctiva of both eyes,
wet. Muscles in her cheeks tightened
against inconsolable grief.
Cigarette burn holes scatter
in the pattern of her night dress.
You see, she's no longer
safe, even though her Emergency Response
System is working well.
She couldn't get to the fire
extinguisher anyway.
The patient is silent.
The space between us, silent.
It takes courage to cry.
No! she chokes out, *I'm giving up.*

Later, at home, I pick up a stone
from the black bowl
on the table. It resembles
part of the human spine separated from body.
I did a good job tightening the bolts
on her wheelchair. I think.

Sarah's Pumpkin Bread

TERRY EVANS *Homer, Alaska*

Working in a doctor's office was very different from working in a hospital. In the office, I learned about the patients, their families, and their hobbies and in some ways felt that I was part of their lives. Some patients I'd see only once or twice, others on a weekly basis — they were the ones I learned to know and love in a personal way during the years I worked in Dr. Collingsworth's office. He was an older doctor who still did things the "old-fashioned" way, even making house calls when necessary. He'd been in the same office for thirty years, and he knew his patients almost as if they were family — some he loved, some he struggled with. But all his patients loved him and trusted him with the healthcare decisions they knew he'd be making throughout the years.

Sarah and Daniel West were such a couple. They were both about seventy years old and lived together in a small apartment just around the corner from the office. Dan had lots of chronic problems — among other things, he was diabetic and had severe heart disease — but Sarah was always there to help him. Whenever Dan's health deteriorated, Dr. Collingsworth put him in the hospital. When he was home again, Dan and Sarah would come by for blood pressure checks and lab work. Often, she'd bake cookies or cakes and bring them over. She was a great baker, and we always enjoyed those snacks during a busy work day.

One day while Dr. Collingsworth was at lunch the receptionist, Edith, and I were alone in the office. We were busy getting things ready for the afternoon appointments when the phone rang. I heard Edith talking, then she called me. "It's Mrs. West. She needs help."

I came to the phone to hear a hysterical Sarah yelling that Dan wasn't breathing.

Trying to remain calm, I said, "Hang up — I'll call an ambulance." After I'd given the emergency operator the patient's name and address, I asked Edith to call Dr. Collingsworth at home.

"Tell him to meet the ambulance at the hospital," I said. "I'm going to the apartment to help Sarah."

I ran out the door, around the back, and down the alley. There were several apartments on the corner. I wasn't sure which one was theirs, but I knew it was number fifteen. I ran through the maze of apartments until I saw Sarah through a window. She was kneeling on the floor.

Opening the front door I called, "Sarah! It's me." Sarah screamed back. "Hurry! He won't breathe!"

I ran through the neat little living room into the small bedroom. Dan was very blue, slumped half-on and half-off the bed. Sarah was beside him, trying to keep him from falling onto the floor. I could hear sirens begin to wail in the distance. Moving Sarah away, I lowered Dan to the floor. He wasn't breathing, and I couldn't find a pulse.

Now my heart was in my throat. I gave him mouth-to-mouth, two big breaths that made his chest rise and fall, then I started chest compressions, one-and-two-and-three-and-four. Puffs, then compressions. Puffs, then compressions, for what seemed like a very long time. He didn't respond, although I thought his cheeks lost some of their dusky blue color. I could see Sarah out of the corner of my eye, wringing her hands and watching. I wanted to hug her, but I was too busy and there was no one else around. The hug would have to be put on hold. I kept up the breathing and the compressions until the ambulance arrived.

When they hooked Dan up to a heart monitor, there was nothing. The bright straight line moved across the monitor screen over and over. One EMT intubated Dan and begin to bag him while another took over CPR. My arms ached and my back was throbbing. They loaded Dan into the ambulance.

Sarah and I got into her small economy car and headed out behind the screaming ambulance that was already disappearing over the hill. I drove fast, trying to catch up.

Dr. Collingsworth was waiting at the ER, and the hospital team had already taken over when we arrived. Dr. Collingsworth, Sarah, and I hugged. Then we stood there holding each other until a doctor — a stranger — came to tell Sarah that Dan was gone. She only hung her head and nodded while we all stood with our arms still around each other. Dr. Collingsworth followed the ER doctor back into the room, and I stood there in that sterile, cold hallway with a woman who, no doubt, felt her world crashing around her.

I thought of the many years that she and Dan had shared. The children they'd raised, the fun times and the hard times, the places they'd seen, the times they'd laughed together and the times they'd cried. I watched as Sarah looked off into space, and I wondered what she was remembering — their wedding day or the day their first child was born? Even when he had been sick, he had been *there*. Now, he was gone.

When she went into the exam room to see Dan, she didn't let go of my hand, just tugged a little so I'd go along with her. He lay still as stone on a small gurney, covered to his neck with a white sheet. He was pale and still slightly blue and very, very still. She walked up to the bedside and stood there gazing at him for a long while. Then, clear and calm, she said, "Thank-you, Dan."

No hysteria, no anger, just "thank-you, Dan."

Thank-you, Dan, for fifty-five years of marriage, for six children, for loving me and always being there for me, for the time I had emergency surgery and you stood beside me while I woke from that awful anesthesia. For the six times you brought me flowers when our kids were born. For the hugs and the pride you shared. For the years of jokes and laughter and loving and caring. Thank-you, Dan. Thank-you for forgiving me, for never holding a grudge when your feelings got hurt. For not laughing when I was embarrassed. For showing me how to fish and then not getting mad when I caught a bigger trout than you did. For asking to learn how to change a diaper, and then doing it. For being a wonderful dad and an even better grandpa. For eating the food I burned and telling me it was perfect. Thanks for telling people you were married to a great lady. For the late night movies and the bowls of popcorn we shared.

"Thank-you, Dan." That's all she said.

We just stood there looking down at this man who was no longer living in his body. She finally kissed him and went to call her children. They all came to her apartment and helped with the funeral arrangements. It was short and simple, because that was what Dan had wanted.

Shortly after that Sarah brought me a loaf of pumpkin bread. She cried that day, standing in the office, and thanked me for being there and not leaving her when she was so alone. I told her I had learned a lot that day, not only about being a nurse, but also about being married. I don't know if she understood that. Not long after, Sarah moved to Los Angeles to be near her son and grandchildren. She died of a heart attack ten years later.

I've made her pumpkin bread recipe often; it always helps me love my job, and my husband, a little more.

Rubbing Her Back at the Nursing Home

MAUREEN TOLMAN FLANNERY *Evanston, Illinois*

The ridge road of her spine
  winds over bluffs.
    The farm itself
      was rough ground,
          required so much stooping,
          bending to stock and soil.
      She gave what it took
  and the daily toil of it
bent her to a hay hook.

Premature

HELEN TRUBEK GLENN *Litchfield, Connecticut*

I am assigned
to bring the infant,
wrapped in a pinned blanket,
to the morgue.
My own pregnancy
bulges against my white uniform.
I push the button for sub-basement,
try to hide the terrible
bundle in my left arm.
I feel the stares, the canny
guesses of older women
on the elevator. They know.
If I could raise my eyes
they would look at me and say,
Think of your own unborn.
But when the door slides open,
my obedient feet
carry me under the hospital,
through glazed ochre
tunnels I have memorized.
I know the formalities,
the courtesies of the morgue.

Eurydice in the State Hospital Laundry

HELEN TRUBEK GLENN *Litchfield, Connecticut*

Sheets boil up fresh in bluing
but the smell of soiled
linen hangs in this steam.
Common laundry.
Inside the collar
I marked my name
in block letters
but my paisley shirtwaist
went to someone else.
I dislike the pink shift
I wear today, put away
in my drawer by mistake.
Where did they put the silks
I designed, lilacs laid over cream
stripes, moiré celadon taffeta?
This washing reduces all fabrics
to clean similarity, uniform
like our faces and shuffling
walk. Tomorrow I will hide
the pill in my cheek.

Portrait

HELEN TRUBEK GLENN *Litchfield, Connecticut*

Your turn from health to illness
visible, the unmade bed
an omen and the brief time
of wearing gaudy colors.

Night bird of feathered
taffeta, iridescent as you turn,
profiled against the light;
life's appetite visible.

Unsound mother, *don't breathe
a word*, turn away, safer,
the disease invisible.
Fear seals part of my throat.

I sell the house with the long
hall, move out the furniture.
The padded table, cleared, holds
the imprint of lifted plates.

Edna's Star

CHRIS GRANT *Penn Valley, Pennsylvania*

The junior year of nursing school is the toughest — too much time invested to back out and too many loans not to continue. It's the year that gives the student a glimpse into a career that could last thirty years or more. During that third year of nursing school, I moved out of the dorm to my first apartment — where I knew I could study better and longer and so become a greater nurse. My apartment was the first floor of an old paper-shingled house; the second-floor apartment above mine seemed to be empty. I didn't know why.

In that third year of nursing, I was learning to "integrate" nursing knowledge. My instructor told me that a second clinical placement in a nursing home would be helpful. After all, nursing theory transcended any client population. I didn't believe it, but given the option of either pass or fail, I went. I didn't have anything against the elderly; I just wasn't ready to work *with* the elderly. I was a much better nurse than they needed. My nursing talent would surely be wasted.

My first assignment was given to me over the phone the night before. I called the nurses' desk and introduced myself. "Oh, you will love Edna," chirped the nurse manager on the other line. She never told me why, and I never asked. I was too focused on the "problem list" I would face.

The day that brought me to Edna changed my nursing life. Edna was hunched over in a faded, rose-colored, upholstered chair when I entered her single room at the end of a yellow-lit corridor. My mind raced as I scanned her room. No IVs, no catheters. I took in the needlepoint chair, which I assumed was urine stained, and I saw a folded walker poised in the corner. It was draped with a homemade cloth "catch-all," and crocheted tissue boxes seemed to be everywhere. The colors were too garish for my taste. Bright pink, purple, and a blue one faded to yellow where fingers had grasped the box too many times. I saw a candy dish with unwrapped mints lying in it (please do not offer me one, I thought to myself), and then finally there was the bed cover —

a lacy, limp, frothy affair. Crocheted. The nursing-home-stamped sheets could be seen through its pattern of holes — perhaps pretty at one time, but no doubt now just a dust catcher — as could Edna's fingers and toes.

Edna never looked at me. She just kept staring at her hands, rubbing the worn fingers and pulling on them, clear out to the tips of the nails as if trying to elongate the gnarly flesh.

"Good morning. I'm your nurse today." I never gave my name, thinking she could read my badge.

Edna traded my insolence with her cold order: "Get my walker." I strode across the room, cool and confident, and returned with the metal frame, setting it down a little too hard in front of her chair. Edna responded with grace, bettering me by choosing to ignore my actions. She reached for the walker, touching the air at first and then landing her fingers on the cool metal. She stood up, shook out her housedress, tugged at the apron she was wearing, and strode out of her room. I watched as she carefully picked her way down the hall. I let her go and turned to her room. I completed all my tasks with mean efficiency. Her bed sheets were pulled tight, her water pitcher refilled, and her crocheted tissue boxes arranged in descending order on her windowsill. Proud of my work, I left the room and moved on to patients who needed my care.

Lunchtime brought the same from Edna. She sat in her chair, rhythmically rubbing her hands as I brought her food tray to her room. Edna apparently preferred to eat by herself. "Lunch," I commanded. Her response again matched mine. "Here," she said and pointed to her lap. As I set the tray on her lap Edna dismissed me with a single gesture of her index finger.

The afternoon brought her nap. I took a look through the door and noted that she had maneuvered her way to the bed, folded back her sheets in the fan style taught only at nursing schools, and pulled her crocheted cover over her tiny frame. Good, I thought to myself. No more dealing with Edna. My shortened, nursing school–type shift ended soon anyway.

Report started. I had my notebook ready. Input, output, lunch tray remains, ambulation — everyone assigned to me was on paper. I was ready.

"How was Edna today?" asked the nurse in charge. Without waiting for an answer she added, "She's going home this afternoon and I'm sure she was so excited." I was stunned into silence. I diverted my eyes to my hands as the nurse continued to speak. "Isn't it amazing how much she can do considering she has just been blinded?" I was quietly horrified. I hadn't known. I hadn't had a clue.

I couldn't wait to escape to my apartment. I could not comprehend how cruel I had been. As I wallowed in self-pity, I heard commotion. The view from my kitchen window was the open wooden stairway that led to the second-floor apartment. I stood at the sink and watched as a middle-aged man started to lug an upholstered chair up the stairs. I couldn't believe the chair would fit up the narrow staircase until I saw the man step back down to the landing and with one mighty swoop put the chair upside down on his head. Up he went, bowed under the weight. My eyes caught the pale faded rose of the chair's seat. *Where had I seen that?* I watched the man bound down the steps. He disappeared for a moment and returned with a diminutive figure attached to one arm and a plastic grocery bag overflowing with clothes in the other. They turned the corner to go up the stairs when I saw her. Edna.

Edna lived above me. I shrank back into my kitchen so she wouldn't see me before I remembered that she couldn't! It was Edna, *blind Edna.*

The man came down the steps again. I waited to hear his return footsteps, but they never came. I realized that Edna was alone. I couldn't move from my kitchen sink. I waited and waited, not knowing what to do. I stood there for a lifetime, then realized I had no choice.

Cautiously I ascended the peeling, warped steps that led to Edna's apartment. My knock on the screen door was almost imperceptible, but a voice responded, "Come in." I pulled back the squeaking screen door and stepped into a dark, tiny kitchen. The gray linoleum floor was worn in front of the sink and the stove; the Formica and metal table was covered with the contents of her cupboards. Everything she needed was in front of her — a radio, jars of preserves, tins of food, boxes of crackers and cereal, plates, cups, spoons, a thermos, and those crocheted tissue boxes. The purple, pink, and even the faded blue cover looked so right in that kitchen on that table. They were perfect. The pale rose chair was pulled up close and there sat Edna.

Edna and I sat at her kitchen table for hours. I made her a cup of tea, opened a can of soup to heat for her supper, and then ran down to my apartment to get my nursing books. I sat at Edna's kitchen table and studied while she quietly listened to the radio. Occasionally I would read a passage out loud to her and she would nod in agreement. We never talked about her health; we never spoke of the nursing home. I was positive she had no idea who I really was.

Each day, I went to Edna's. My mornings began at her kitchen table, sharing bowls of cereal. My evenings ended as I watched her pull her crocheted coverlet up to her chin. Edna and I talked about everything. I would read her the paper; she would tell me a story she had heard on the radio. I would boil the water for tea and she would get out her best china cups. I picked up her groceries when I got mine. I allowed myself the luxury of denial regarding my initial meeting of Edna, and she had the grace not to remember. Our gentle friendship grew quickly.

As the week came to a close I was placed on an afternoon clinical rotation. I forgot to tell Edna that my schedule would change for the next few weeks. But I knew we would have our mornings and early afternoons together. Following a long day on a new rotation, I arrived home late. I glanced up at Edna's apartment and saw only darkness. Edna must be asleep, I thought. Minutes later, I was too.

The next morning I rushed to get my coffee and ran up the steps to see Edna. I arrived at the top landing a little winded and knocked my quiet signal on the screen door. No answer. I peered through the glass, through the limp, lace curtains. Edna's chair was gone.

The spring of my graduation year arrived. I was excited to become a nurse at last — a good one, I thought, but probably not great. Edna had taught me that. I'd thought of Edna a lot during my final year in nursing school, and I missed her.

While I was getting ready for graduation, the mail carrier left a small package at my door. It was wrapped in brown paper, tied with string. No return address.

I undid the wrapping and opened the box. Lying on yellowed tissue paper was a crocheted cloth. I carefully took it out of the box and opened it on my table. A star. An eight-pointed star. A star beautifully crocheted, starched and white, burst open on my table.

Tears filled my eyes as my fingers smoothed the delicate knots. My hands shook as I opened the note left inside the box: *My mother made this for you. This star was the last and only thing she crocheted after becoming blind. She said it was for the eight days you cared for her. She said you were a good nurse from day one, but the best nurse by day eight.*

Twenty-six years later, Edna's eight-pointed star is still on my table. And every day I am reminded that becoming the best nurse possible starts with being just a good nurse.

Conversation with Wendy

AMY HADDAD *Omaha, Nebraska*

We dream
our hair is long,
longer than it has ever been.
Long and red,
long and brown,
hanging in our faces,
rustling past our ears,
silky and impossibly shiny.

When she got the news
she went straight home,
took shears and chopped away her red hair,
shaved the rest with electric clippers.
She covers her bald head
with fuchsia turbans and blue scarves.

I held on to mine.
Walking to my car
on a beautiful fall day,
absently pushing hair out of my eyes,
a handful came loose,
trailing from my fingers.
On the drive home
I couldn't leave it alone.
Long brown strands
flew from my hand
out the car window,
glinting in the sun.

I hid in a wig in public,
threw it on the dining room table
the minute I got home.

Wendy still rides the roller coaster of chemo,
up and down, on and off,
sometimes off long enough
for red fuzz to grow back.
Friends gave her money to buy a wig.
She bought a lhasa apso puppy instead,
and wears scarves.

My hair grew back slowly,
gray and strangely coarse.
I keep it cropped close to my head.

Port-a-Cath

AMY HADDAD *Omaha, Nebraska*

Button made of skin,
easy access to my veins.
Easy as a whore,
blank-eyed and indifferent,
opening to the syringe.

When chemo is through,
I ask to have it removed.
The silver scar stays
peeking out above my bra,
shining at dinner parties.

Ten Items or Less

AMY HADDAD *Omaha, Nebraska*

I can spot them
even in the checkout line.
Putting the rubber stick
between their oranges and my bread,
I see hands
marked with purple, green,
and yellow bruises.
I know where they have been,
the needle sticks just the start of it.

The bruise tattoos,
each prick leaving its history.
I match the hand to the face
looking for signs of what is killing them
as they sort coupons
for cereal or canned tomatoes.

Tet, Vietnam 1968

PAULINE HEBERT *Rainbow Lake, New York*

A litter dropped onto sawhorses
at the far end of Triage, another nameless
boy, one of hundreds this day.

I nurse you as you lay dying.
The sight of your swollen face
sears into my mind forever.

Your head swaddled
in layer upon layer of dressings,
all bright red, hemorrhaging blood.

Blood that clots, mingles
amid jungle grasses
that share your bed.

Through the litter's canvas,
audible steady drips of blood
settle on my boots.

The Story of Mr. President

NINA HOWES *New York, New York*

When I worked at the county hospital there was this nurse who was into the punk thing. She would show up with her white platform shoes, her white miniskirt, and her white head band. Her name was Kiki and she really was a good nurse; she had a big heart. One day, she was walking down the hall with one of her patients whose name was Mr. President. He was holding onto his IV, and she was holding him by the other arm. Another patient called to her, so she turned away for a few minutes. Meanwhile, Mr. President kept walking. When she finished the conversation, she looked around. Mr. President had taken off and was heading for an open window. "Mr. President," she called. "Mr. President," but he wouldn't stop. "Mr. President!" she yelled and chased after him, trying to run in her white platform shoes. He was about to throw himself out the window, the IV dangling off his arm, when she reached out and grabbed him by the legs. So now he was hanging out the window, she was holding onto his legs, and a nurse's aide rushed over and grabbed onto her. It looked like something out of a Charlie Chaplin movie. Finally, Mr. President was too heavy and Kiki couldn't hold onto him anymore. He fell. A few minutes later, the phone rang. It was the engineering department. "Did you lose a patient?" they asked. Apparently, engineering was doing some construction work on the grounds near the window, and Mr. President had conveniently fallen into a soft mound of dirt. "He's doing all right," they added. "He just needs to get cleaned up a bit." Mr. President came back to the floor, and Kiki rushed over and gave him a big hug, dirt and all. I'll never forget that image of her chasing him down the hall yelling, "Mr. President! Mr. President!" as if she were at some White House press conference.

Age Garden

KAREN HOWLAND *Milwaukee, Wisconsin*

1.

A boy's head butters the tops of petals
with young blond sun. This four-year-old Icarus
flies off picnic tables, trees, bikes.
His running is yeast. His sticky hands
are spiders that eat the sky. His curiosity
chases the wagon on a red-winged blackbird.
Bee-stung by silence, he shouts *You're it*
to the peonies, poppies, foxglove, and dogwood.
He is a pink pepper up and down.
A blueberry lost to cheek and joy.
His skin is honey and piano.
His scraped knee sings tomatoes and baseballs.

2.

That August afternoon often finds its way
into the wrinkles, pills, and spokes
of a chair with wheels. A man pretends
his pain is a radish, his arthritis
has actually turned his hands into spiders.
He still eats the sky when the nurse opens his window.
Bee-stung by silence, he wants to shout but can't
catch his breath running up and down bone, throat, and lung.
He learns to run faster than light without moving
in bed. Roses started clotting his blood
and, one day, broke free, rose to his brain,
blooming summer so fully all other thought
stopped.

3.

No one ever guessed about the garden
growing beneath the sheet
or the boy playing hide and seek
under the white daisies of his hair.

The Teacher

HILARIE JONES *Manchester, Connecticut*

I was twenty-six the first time I held
a human heart in my hand.

It was sixty-four and heavier than I expected,
its chambers slack;
and I was stupidly surprised
at how cold it was.

It was the middle of the third week
before I could look at her face,
before I could spend more than an hour
learning the secrets of cirrhosis,
the dark truth of diabetes, the black lungs
of the Marlboro woman, the exquisite
painful shape of kidney stones,
without eating an entire box of Altoids
to smother the smell of formaldehyde.

After seeing her face, I could not help
but wonder if she had a favorite color;
if she hated beets,
or loved country music before her hearing
faded, or learned to read
before cataracts placed her in perpetual twilight.
I wondered if her mother had once been happy
when she'd come home from school
or if she'd ever had a valentine from a secret admirer.

In the weeks that followed, I would
drive the highways, scanning billboards.
I would see her face, her eyes
squinting away the cigarette smoke,
or she would turn up at the bus stop
pushing a grocery cart of empty

beer cans and soda bottles. I wondered
if that was how she'd paid for all those smokes
or if the scars of repeated infections in her womb
spoke to a more universal currency.

Did she die, I wondered, in a cardboard box
under the Burnside Bridge, nursing a bottle
of strawberry wine, telling herself
she felt a little warmer now,
or in the Good Faith Shelter,
her few belongings safe under the sheet
held to her faltering heart?
Or in the emergency room, lying
on a wheeled gurney, the pitiless
light above, the gauzy curtains around?

Did she ever wonder what it all was for?

I wish I could have told her in those days
what I've now come to know: that
it was for this — the baring
of her body on the stainless steel table —
that I might come to know its secrets
and, knowing them, might listen
to the machine-shop hum of aortic stenosis
in an old woman's chest, smile a little to myself
and, in gratitude to her who taught me,

put away my stethoscope, turn to my patient
and say, *Let's talk about your heart.*

At the Beginning of Each Shift

ALYSON KENNEDY *Santa Cruz, California*

At the beginning of each shift,
I dive into the deepest end of the pool.
All ropes and side ladders have been withdrawn.
Doggie-paddle, breaststroke, back float —
anything to keep my head above water.
Underneath, churning riptides pummel my body,
strong currents surge against me,
carrying away a myriad of tasks.
Bobbing erratically like a damaged cork,
I know immersion is inevitable.

I open my eyes underwater
and look through the watery veil to the midnight sky.
I whisper the names of the stars I know:
Sirius, Procyon, Pollux, Castor, Aldebaran, Rigel.
They roll off my tongue like an alchemist's plea.
I stretch my fingers out of the water
and trace these starry dots,
connecting unthinkable distances
to form a design that saves me.
Slipping my arms through this brilliant life ring,
I am able to breathe.

Like a Night Watchman

ALYSON KENNEDY *Santa Cruz, California*

Like a night watchman composed by vigilance
I walk up and down this corridor.
Peering into each patient's room,
I shine my tiny penlight,
searching for perilous harbingers.
But my light is blunted, darkness
acts as a mordant, fixing me to the night.

The floor is dulled where my nurse shoes
have tread back and forth like errant pilgrims.
I have traveled the circumference of the earth
without ever having left this carpeted isthmus
between uncertainty and relief.

Then I see you, Moon,
secured tightly to the night sky
by gauzy strips of cloud.
You look like a big blue pearl
tethered and trussed by the oyster's flesh,
unable to nudge or meet your destiny
as a roving sphere.

You fool me, Moon.
As each hour of my shift dissolves into the coming light,
I track your transit from window pane to window pane,
revealing your journey, my journey.

The Facts of Lice
in Nueva Vida, Nicaragua

SUE KLASSEN *Managua, Nicaragua*

"Sandra has *gripe*," her mother, Angela, told me, explaining that her cough, cold, and occasional fever had been going on for over two weeks. I asked some more questions and was going to examine Sandra when Angela interrupted. "Oh and by the way, *mira*," she said, "see, Sandra also has some sores on her head."

Angela fingered through Sandra's hair to show me. I examined her head too and thought her shoulder-length hair would walk right off her scalp. Every millimeter of each shaft of hair was crawling with lice, and her scalp was peppered with eggs and caked with scabs. I'd seen lice when my eight-year-old daughter had come home from school with an itchy head. And I'd thought *that* was bad.

Eleven-year-old Sandra had come to the clinic with her mother and two younger sisters, Flor, age eight, and baby Kandi. Sandra's and Flor's school uniforms were untucked, askew, and the girls looked as sweaty and grimy as I felt on this humid, dusty day. Angela's shoulders slumped wearily while naked Kandi squirmed on her lap.

I knew why Angela was so fatigued that afternoon. Nueva Vida is a community of about 14,000 people who relocated here to start a new life after Hurricane Mitch flooded their lakefront homes in October, 1998. Displaced to tiny houses on small plots of land, fifteen miles away from the lake where they earned their livelihoods as fisher-people, these Nicaraguans were desperately poor. Angela probably spent her morning waiting her turn at the neighborhood water faucet, scrubbing piles of laundry by hand, cooking red beans over an open wood fire, and tending to the baby.

Jubilee Clinic, situated in the center of Nueva Vida, had been started by a North American based non-governmental organization soon after this new *barrio* was formed. Fifteen months ago, I had joined Jorge, a family physician; Henry, a medical technician; and Maria, the gatekeeper who determined who would be seen each day, cleaned the floors and, as a resident of the community, seemed to know everything about everyone.

Thanks to the frequent donations we received, we had Nix shampoo on hand. I explained to Angela that it would be best to cut Sandra's hair as short as possible and give it a rigorous washing before using the special shampoo. I also emphasized the importance of good hygiene and other preventive measures.

About ten days later, wondering how Sandra was doing, I asked Maria to send word for her to stop by and see me after school. I shouldn't have been surprised, but was, to see her stringy hair still in motion. I decided a home visit was in order.

I went accompanied by Maria and Christine, a Canadian volunteer whose hair was shaved off — her style of choice. We walked the four blocks to Sandra's house, stepping around trash piles and water-filled potholes, greeted by passers-by along the way. Armed with gloves, scissors, anti-lice shampoo and lots of good humor, we were ready to tackle Sandra's embarrassing situation.

Like the hundreds around it, Sandra's house was a small, one-room cement block structure divided in the middle by a curtain that separated living room from bedroom. The dirt floor was neatly swept. Sparse belongings were nicely arranged on a small table in the back corner. We were led past a patch of pink and white Impatiens and a struggling rose bush to the side yard. By this time Flor, with whom Sandra shared a bed, also had lice.

First, Angela scrubbed the girls' hair by dipping water out of a big barrel and pouring it over their heads. Then, after she gave me her permission, the girls elected me to be hair cutter. With the others cheering me on, I cut shorter and shorter.

It was 5:30 by the time we got back to the clinic. We were closing up and about to hop into the car when crew-cut Sandra came running into the clinic, baby Kandi slung on her hip. Sandra was crying. It seemed that her stepfather had just returned home from fishing and, furious about the haircuts, was threatening to beat Angela. My good deed had incited family violence.

Henry told Sandra that clinic staff couldn't interfere with domestic matters, but Maria and I agreed to return home with her. Back at the house, Maria tried to reason with Antonio, who was scaling a pile of Tilapia fish out back in the kitchen hut.

"How dare you cut my daughters' hair without asking my permission?" he demanded. "Who do you think is in charge of this house anyway?"

Maria's calm reassurance that his daughters' hair had been cut to help their health was to no avail. Meanwhile, I attempted to console Angela, who was cowering at the front door and weeping as the three girls clung to her tattered skirt. Antonio had followed through on similar threats enough times in the past. She knew he was serious.

"Que vergüenza!" Antonio ranted on. "How shameful for others to see my daughters with such hairdos. People will think they are ill with something contagious and will not want to buy the fish they need to sell for me!" Of course, the fact that the fish from Lake Managua were contaminated with heavy metals from nearby industrial plants didn't change the fact that fishing was his livelihood; his fish had to be sold.

I don't know if Angela was beaten that night or not. She did accept my suggestion to meet with the clinic counselor, and later I heard she got a court order forcing Antonio to leave their home. I was glad Angela had the courage to protect herself and her children, but I wondered how she would provide for her family. I even tried to feel compassion for Antonio, who showed up at the clinic with several big cuts across his face and hand. He said robbers assaulted him. Maria said he'd been tussling with his drinking buddies.

The next time I saw Sandra and Flor, their heads were free of lice at last. Their eyes sparkled and they grinned shyly as they put on the navy blue Nike baseball caps I had brought them. "Que linda!" I exclaimed, winking. "How pretty you are." They glanced at each other, nodded in agreement, and skipped out the door.

Stethoscope

SHIRLEY KOBAR *Aurora, Colorado*

You frighten us
with your hollowed cheeks,
grating breath sounds,
a petri dish of disease.
We probe with extensions of ourselves,
no longer anointing with pungent oils
or healing with the laying on of hands.
We are far from René Laënnec,
who safeguarded himself from indelicacy
with his rolled paper.
We use elongated tubes to listen
to the universe,
shielding us from bodily humors,
contact with skin to skin,
breath to breath.

Mourning Coffee

JOAN STACK KOVACH *Budapest, Hungary*

Down the hall from the Emergency Room is the family room with its green leather and wood chairs, a settee, end tables, low table lamps that are on in spite of the harsh hospital overhead lights, a phone, a small pad of paper, and a pen. Sometimes, when I come to work an evening shift, there's a tray with a white coffee carafe, Styrofoam cups, a plate of cookies, a paper bowl of creamers, sugar, Sweet 'N Low, and shiny brown plastic stirring sticks, just there, untouched. The scavenger in me, the part of me that hates waste and wants to use and reuse everything, has learned to look in a few times when I walk by the family room to see if, after a while, all those things are still there. When it seems that no one is using the room anymore, I scarf up the coffee and cookies, taking a cookie from the plate to leave on my desk for later in the shift when I'll need it and pouring myself a cup of coffee if I'm so inclined. I present the rest to the harried staff in the ER, placing it on the counter near the fracture room and beds 5 through 10.

"Oh, who brought this?"

"Where did these come from?"

"Oatmeal raisin? Any chocolate chip?" they ask, not expecting answers. They help themselves as they rush by, busy, hungry, no need to know. Or perhaps they do already know the source of this unexpected refreshment; it's mourning coffee, brought over from the family room before dietary could reclaim it or housekeeping toss it out. We might make small talk about the cookies, but we don't talk about why they are there.

Mourning coffee — like the chaplain, the liaison nurse, and the doctor cloaked in white with bad news to tell — is what the hospital can offer to the families of someone who has died. The tall white plastic carafe sitting alone and elegant in the empty room means that earlier in the day a family crossed over from being worried about the living to trying to accept the fact of death. The coffee, the cookies, the phone, the special staff, and the room do their best to hold and support the grieving. They all bear witness to the grief, be it loud, wailing, resistant, wild and dangerous, or soft, gentle, and weeping grief or stoic, stifled, and blank. The firm walls, constant furniture, and steady staff hold people at a time when what is real is too enormous to be held alone. Sometimes the cups are used, the coffee is poured, the cookies half eaten but likely not tasted. They are tangible kindnesses that help to fill the cracks in the universe that come with a death. They are solid, immovable as boulders, a sure thing to rest against as one absorbs the fact that leaving, too, is part of life.

The first time I saw the pot of coffee and figured out why it was there, it felt spooky, the way a cemetery can feel when each stone represents a story you don't know but fear. Death by its very existence scares us, makes us worry that we can become more susceptible to it, just by acknowledging it. Up close to death, or very far away from it, we somehow feel safer. But to know only that someone has died — that someone had to hear that a loved one was gone, perhaps even had to watch the doctor put his defeated hands in his lab coat pockets as he left the room, perhaps had to accept the embrace of a careful, kind chaplain they may never have seen before — even knowing about that can be, well, scary. Why should that be? Death is common, natural, inevitable. Perhaps. But it is also unreal, unacceptable, and unfathomable. So how can we know it better? Understand it more and fear it less? How can we spend time with people who know about death? Aren't they by definition inaccessible to us?

Last year I attended the memorial service of a kind man I knew from church. Sumner knew he was dying, knew there would be a service, knew those in attendance could use his help. On the back of the order of service for his memorial there was a note from him, acknowledging his understanding of how we might feel, sitting there in the pew waiting for things to begin. How warm and friendly he made it for us by taking the time to prepare.

Sometimes, you know ahead of time; sometimes, it is sudden and one you know or love is just gone. Then there are all those long, long days of looking at and sorting through all the things they couldn't take with them, those things that remind us of them, that make the holes created by their eternal absence so huge.

I once heard two friends who suffered such losses talking about the cemetery where their loved ones were buried, as if it were a new neighborhood they were discovering.

"Did you see the balloons on the grave up near the fence?"

"Yes. Who could that be?"

"I don't know. Aren't they all singles?"

"Right, so no one's moved in recently . . ."

"Maybe they were for the girl who's been there twenty years."

Their conversation was, to me, an indication of their triumph over the awful assault of their losses, of their new connection — not disconnection — with the dead.

I've heard it said that death is just a major change of address. This comforts me and makes working with dying patients less scary. People do move, and it hurts, and we miss them madly. Thinking of the dead as somewhere else, even if we can't write or visit, helps. When my niece died, my brother offered the image of her "in heaven bringing Pop Pop a cup of coffee." That image helped.

A palm reader once told me that we all travel in love packs, stuck together for one lifetime and then reassembled in the next, same characters with the roles changed. I like that too. Maybe our bodies don't last forever, but our connections do. Maybe the coffee prepared for the grieving and consumed by the harried is one way that the connections keep going.

Endurance and Faith

DEBRA KOWALSKI *Willimantic, Connecticut*

After three months working as an RN in a Boston teaching hospital, I'd developed a morning ritual for the elevator ride up to Foster Seven. First, I checked my shoes. A few gray scuffs; I'd polish them tomorrow. A run starting at the ankle of my stockings; I'd pick up a new pair over the weekend. The faint red-brown of an iodine stain near the pocket of my uniform; I'd never really get it out.

The elevator rumbled higher. Ping—Foster Four. Check the pockets: bandage scissors, okay; Kelly clamp, okay; mini-flashlight, okay; one roll of adhesive tape, one black pen, one multicolored pen, okay. Mental check: cigarettes in my bag, stethoscope, money for lunch if I get lucky enough to eat. Okay.

Ping—Foster Six. My heart beating faster. My hand over my nursing pin. (I don't care if I eat, really, I'd say to myself—I only need what's written on the pin: Endurance. Faith.)

Ping—Foster Seven. Walk out of the elevator, okay, okay, okay.

You'll be okay.

I turned left into the hallway. Tom was in the first room, a twenty-year-old diabetic. His fingers had blackened and shriveled like wet leather gloves mistakenly left on the radiator to dry. Tom mostly talked about playing his guitar, but his fingers died before he did, deserting him, lying in white bandages, waiting. After a while, Tom didn't talk much about anything. He kept to his bed.

When assignments were passed out, I silently hoped that I wouldn't be his primary nurse. Please. I'll take any patient, but not Tom. Sometimes I'd stop before I got to his doorway and lean against the wall and concentrate very hard. I'd pray that someone knew how to help Tom, how to comfort him. I didn't know what to do for him.

At the entrance to the next room, I could smell chemotherapy, the acrid, metallic smells that ooze from pores and saturate urine: Cytoxan, Oncovin, Methotrexate. Names for the smells of destruction. Then there were the nameless, experimental chemicals, tubes and bottles wrapped in foil to shield the cell-blasters from light. Chemotherapy versus cancer, foul and lethal competitors, the patient a victim of both as the battle wore on.

Another patient, Gina, got the cell-blasters. I smoothed what was left of her hair— chick fluff— off her clammy forehead. Her gums bled, her rectum bled. The nurses couldn't give her pain medication with a needle for fear that a hemorrhage would start inside her muscle. We hoped for a break in her delirium so she could swallow a pill without choking.

As I leaned over her one morning to adjust the ties of a fresh johnny, she grabbed my wrist and said with absolute clarity, "What does your pin say?"

I was startled, and leaned back quickly to see her face.

"It says, 'Endurance and Faith,' Gina."

"Likely story," Gina mumbled. She faded back into confusion with a smile on her face.

When her cell count dropped so low that she was without immunological defense, I gowned, masked, and gloved to protect her. I recited the daily news while I cared for her, as if she understood every word. I'd sign off before I left with a whispered, "'Endurance and Faith,' Gina." I could give her the words, even if I wasn't sure that they worked for me.

It was a different Gina who eventually left the floor. She was subdued, older, it seemed, than her thirty years. But Gina was discharged alive.

Helen was forty and came to Foster Seven after having a mastectomy. Her cancer had metastasized and the prognosis was poor. Following an unsuccessful course of radiation, Helen asked that further treatment be stopped. This was the only time I heard her make a firm request. She never voiced the range of emotions we'd come to expect— fear, anger, sadness.

"Debbie," she said softly one morning after I had bathed her, "on your next pass by, could you bring me pain medication?" I had noticed her wincing when I turned her to make the bed, and her breakfast had gone uneaten.

"You didn't eat anything, Helen."

"Oh, I'm not very hungry in the morning," she replied.

"What is your favorite food, the one you like most?"

She smiled faintly. "Ice cream."

I consulted with the dietician. "Well, she can't have ice cream for breakfast. It's not nutritious," was the reply. No amount of reasoning would convince her to send anything but the gray gruel I'd seen on the tray. So the next morning I brought in maple walnut ice cream for Helen to eat with her tea, and I had the pain injection ready before her bath. *Anticipate, ask questions*, those were my strategies. And yet I worried that something would be left undone because it had gone unspoken.

On several occasions I'd tried to guess Helen's thoughts, her feelings about her life and her hospitalization, but her eyes moved away from mine and my probing felt like sacrilege. The less Helen needed, the more the nurses tried to do. It was our bond with her.

Helen's husband, Jack, needed us a great deal. He told us stories about his life with Helen and described the A-frame he had finished building for her after all the lean years. We came to know the Helen reflected back to us in Jack's love. Maybe this was the only Helen we really knew. We cared for her as our mother, our sister, our friend. Jack came loaded each morning with boxes of donuts, chocolates, and fresh tangerines. He offered to drive us to and from the hospital if we needed a ride. While Helen was resting, Jack sat in the nurses' report room handing out donuts and coffee, catching a piece of conversation here, a bit of news there, as we ran in and out and wolfed a donut or snatched a drag on a cigarette. We were always on the run, but Jack understood. He and Helen had crossed hospital borders.

On a cold December morning, Helen vomited, quietly, the way she did everything, her breakfast tea rolling out as if she were surrendering her last physical attachment to the world. I cleaned her carefully, gently cradling and lifting her to change the bed. Her olive skin felt soft beneath my hands. I knew the angle of her cheekbone against my arm and the texture of the dark brown hair that fell across her face. Her slender body seemed heavy, her limbs slack, and she responded sluggishly to my ministrations. Laying her back on the bed, I thought, *Helen is dying*.

I wanted to be there with her, the bond unbroken, until I was sure that Helen would need me no more. But six other patients waited for me outside that room. One was Tracy. Left with right-sided paralysis after a stroke, he could understand words spoken to him but was unable to communicate. Tracy needed complete assistance to eat, to urinate, to move. The only bodily function

Tracy controlled was his breathing. He could take a breath without me.

Then there was Dorie with advanced pancreatic cancer. Her stomach could no longer digest food, and so bottles of nutrients were pumped into her subclavian vein. Uncontrollable diarrhea excoriated her edematous thighs. She required clockwork pain medication and the reassurance that she'd receive that medication at regular intervals and not be kept waiting.

Don was another patient, a "train wreck" with multisystem failure. When he'd gone into heart failure, his kidneys failed too; then further complications developed throughout his body, a pileup of interrelated problems. How long had it been since I'd checked on him? I had to be sure his machines were working; I had to know what signs and symptoms might signal trouble. Was Don becoming more restless? Had his color changed? Was his last sentence poetic, or was he confused? And I had three other patients that I hadn't seen. One of them required insulin before breakfast. Breakfast was finished.

"Helen," I whispered, as I knelt at her bedside and stroked her cheek. "I have to go to my other patients. I'll be back soon."

I was back in ten minutes. When I entered Helen's room, she was exactly as I had posed her, turned on her side, facing the door. Yesterday, her body had molded warm hollows and fitful ridges in the sheets, but now the sun spread evenly across the bed. My hand slid down the curve of her neck and stopped. I waited for the tapping of her heart against my fingertips. Frosted crystals clung to the window, their patterns changing as the sun returned first one, and then another, to water. My fingers dug deeper into cord and muscle. My mouth dried.

The room seemed to darken then, the winter sun withdrawing. My hand dropped. Trails of water etched the window.

A dull light blinked insistently on the chrome bed rail, rousing me like an unwelcome alarm. Turning, I saw the call light from across the hall firing in silent urgency. Out of habit, I moved to the room. Dorie was grasping the metal triangle over her bed trying to lift herself up enough to ease the pressure on her back. Her lips were compressed, her face taut. "Where have you been?" she asked, her voice high and strained.

"Dorie," I said, "a woman just died." I held onto the metal bar that suspended the triangle. Dorie's fingers slackened and she collapsed back on the bed, shrinking into herself as if she had been suddenly deflated.

What had I said? You never brought another death into a patient's room unless they invited it — most rooms were already full. When was Dorie's last pain medication? I couldn't remember. I looked at my watch. 8:30 A.M. How long had I been in Helen's room? I didn't know. It was one of my nightmares — when I couldn't provide overdue medication, when time kept passing and nothing got done, when no matter how hard I tried it was just too late.

Jack continued to visit us after Helen's death. He brought the same donuts, candy, and coffee, and sat with us in the nurses' room. It seemed that Jack had nowhere else to go. We'd been his buddies during the siege. We knew how it was for him, but still, we were always on the run. Jack didn't understand. His face crumpled into an expression of bewildered anguish.

The staff invited Jack to the floor's Christmas party held at my apartment. I sat next to him while he gulped vodka and tonic as if he couldn't quench his thirst. "I wanted to take her home. I could have cared for her there." He looked at his chafed, weathered hands, the hands of a carpenter. There is a kind of grief — raw and bottomless — that nothing spoken can assuage. So I spoke only to let Jack know that I was present, that he was not talking to himself.

"Did Helen ever say anything about dying?"

"No, she talked about —," he cleared his throat, "— about plans for her garden, vacations we would take, what colors to paint the rooms. Three years ago, before her first chemotherapy, when the doctor told her the cancer had spread, she made jokes about being a cue ball, about how I could autograph her head when her hair fell out. I left the room, went to the kitchen so she wouldn't see me cry. That's when I thought she wasn't going to make it. A few days before she died she said to me, 'You'll be okay.'"

He patted his knee and stared toward the top of the Christmas tree where a white star glowed.

Each of us hugged Jack before he left the party. I wasn't sure that he would be okay. Despite his foreboding, he'd believed Helen's plans for a future that included them both. I stood on the outside steps and watched Jack walk down the street, hands stuffed in his pockets, snow falling on his bent head. From behind me, "O Come All Ye Faithful" drifted into the darkness.

Toward the end of my first year, after Helen's death, I began to suspect that something was wrong with the system. Too many days were filled with impossible choices, too many nights were spent first going over the details of care I had given to patients to be sure I hadn't missed something, then trying to purge the events of the shift so I could relax enough to sleep.

One afternoon I found Sally, my friend and one of the best nurses on the floor, crying at the end of the hall, her knuckles pressed into her mouth. Her patient had pulled out his urinary catheter, and she was already behind. "Why didn't you ask me for help?" I asked, knowing the answer already. There were many un-spoken taboos; asking for help was one of them. Sally had become my role model for survival; I figured if she could do it, then so could I. But as Sally clutched herself, her freckles wet, the white cap lopsided on her curly brown hair, I decided we'd had enough. I was going for help.

First I went to the head nurse, who watched the smoke from her cigarette disappear into the air while I explained how I felt about the workload.

"But you're doing a fine job," she said. "Just do the best you can. Don't get so involved."

I bypassed the supervisor.

After writing a four-page letter to the director of nursing, I received a summons to her office. This was the first time I had seen her since orientation when she had told us how, back in her day, nurses used a pulley to send the single thermometer between floors.

"I was very moved by your letter," the director began, then proceeded to tell me how the millions of dollars in the hospital budget were allocated. At first I was flattered that she'd discuss these matters with me casually, as if we were equals. But then I felt like Alice falling through the looking glass into a disordered world. I knew human needs and human pain — that was where I worked. The information she gave me made no sense, and I had no language to grasp it. I stared at the strand of pearls around her neck, each pearl connected to the next, each contributing its own luster to the whole. And then I imagined the strand breaking, the pearls scattering in every direction, each diminished in its solitary space. Leaving the office, I dimly comprehended that we hadn't communicated.

The staffing levels on Foster Seven continued as they had been, and I had dreams of falling, dreams of being chased, dreams of riots.

"You're grinding your teeth at night," my new dentist pronounced mournfully. He asked, "Is there anything I should know?"

Yes, I wanted to say, there is. I am the girl with the glass jaw for whom pain is a reminder of my patients' pain, of the patients I can't reach in time, of the Helens who die without me.

"No," I said. "There is nothing."

My transfer to Farrell Three, a psychiatric unit, has been accepted. I gather with the staff on Foster Seven and Sally presents me with a green dress trimmed with gold buttons as a farewell gift. I won't be wearing a white uniform on Farrell Three. The nurses ask me repeatedly if I am sure that I like the dress. I do. Finally, to prove it, I put the dress on and model it for them as we all look into the long mirror in the nurses' room, their hands touching me, their faces watching my reaction.

"This dress, it's the greatest," I say, fingering the buttons and smoothing the skirt. And so we say good-bye with touch — the language we know best.

That night, I remember how, when I was fourteen, I'd telephoned the local hospital to ask if I could be a candy striper. I loved that pink and white uniform and the way my white shoes cushioned each step so that I walked quietly, as if on air, down the shining hospital floors. The smell of bleach and antiseptic were comforting, the smell of sanctuary, where people were protected, healed.

My next uniform was pink, the color of the nurse's aide. I wrote long notes in the patients' charts when the shift was finished, suggesting to the doctors what I thought my patients needed. Some of the nurses tittered when they read those notes, but I imagined we were partners, all working toward the same goal.

Now, folding my white uniforms into a box, I pack them on top of the white shoes, cracked and scuffed. I add my nickel-plated bandage scissors and my stethoscope, the special one I'd ordered so that heart sounds would be more clear. I lift the uniforms and tuck my name pin with the initials RN deep into one of the shoes. Only my nursing pin remains. Turning it around in the light, I look at it as though for the first time. Below a bronzed relief, the pin bears the inscription, "Endurance and Faith."

"Endurance and Faith," I whisper to myself over and over, as if the words are a mantra. Then I nestle the pin in the box.

"Endurance," I say before closing the lid. "Just endurance."

Four Men, Sitting

SCOTT CHISHOLM LAMONT *Albuquerque, New Mexico*

I pause for a moment
and look up
from your chart,
the litany of your final night,
the litany I am authoring.

They are four men, sitting.

I watch them
watching you:
father,
uncle,
godfather,
and friend in faith.

Eyes red with fatigue,
lips moving in prayer,
they sit in a line
beside your bed.

Their love for you
is palpable;
it fills this room,
fills my world.

At the center of my world,
the center of their world,
is you.

You are surrounded
and dwarfed
by the equipment
that keeps your heart beating.

Your picture smiles down
upon a boy
who no longer looks
like you.

Your bed is filled
with toys
your little brother sent.

I have placed each toy
with care:
a truck
holds heavy tubing in place.
A spaceship
keeps your hand curled
in its natural form.

The four men, sitting,
watch the rise
and fall
of your chest.

They watch as urine
pours relentlessly
from your body
through a tube.

They watch the drain
in your head
that can no longer help you.

They watch the monitor's
shifting numbers,
quickly learning
to understand,
as all families do here.

Each night
I have fought to bend

those numbers
into a different story.

Each night, without fail,
these four men have held your hand,
stroked your hair,
and prayed.

Each night,
they have asked me
not to cease
my efforts to save you
and, until now,
I have not.

This moment is different.

This moment
I felt the change.

Now I fight
to pass your life on,
to give these four hearts
and all the others
that surround you
the time and peace
to say good-bye.

Tomorrow,
I will rest,
no longer intervening,
no longer writing
of each care-filled act.

Tomorrow, someone else will live,
someone else will see,
someone else will grow,
because of your life
and your family's love.

Tomorrow,
only a few moments away.

The last few moments
of your six years.

I have so much still to do.

So many tiny details,
a string of moments and acts
that will turn your life
into many.

But for now,
for just one moment,
one bright, frail moment,
we are five men, sitting
with you.

Not Mine

SCOTT CHISHOLM LAMONT *Albuquerque, New Mexico*

My colleagues
tell me of the ones
who got to them:
a preschooler
too much like their own,
or a baby
reminiscent of a treasured niece.
Many leave.
Many avoid nursing kids entirely.

They tell me I'm lucky
I have none.
No little one to fear for,

no pretuned heart strings.
Each fragile form that comes
into my care —
not mine.

I don't feel
lucky.

Old Man in Bedclothes

JEANNE LEVASSEUR *Columbia, Connecticut*

Maybe you think no one is under these blankets,
just an old man who barely breaks
the swell of bedclothes in a hot
square room where the long afternoon

blisters. You think *he* is nearly gone from this skeleton
and these fingers that *pick pick* at the covers.
Maybe he is smoke,
on the shoulder of the mountain.
His old limbs are so mottled
and gray, they are like green baize poplars the belling
forest calls down all around him.
Soon he will be thistledown,
leaftip
or the whistle

between pine needles. Who can stop him?
His mouth drooping: He is not
blueberries *plunk plunk* in the pail
or the cream jug beside the blue china.
He is god's breath. He is the dustbowl,
he is everything beginning.

Our bowed heads are so somber.
We are made of next to nothing, moisture
on the upper lip, fluids
in our dark rocking parts. Soon what is left will uncouple

and lift to air.
Cathedrals are opening their doors,
his milky eyes focus back once,
then he is gone, like a sail
creaking out to sea. Gone, like a window
opening in August.

Redemption at the Women's Center

JEANNE LEVASSEUR *Columbia, Connecticut*

She swings her legs and kicks the table hard.
Her man's been stepping out.
She's heard he has a baby by another woman.
A pin could drop.
That should be her baby.
She licks her lips. Dust.
And the itch *down there* venereal.
Sweet Jesus, she wanted to be someone.
Be someone. Didn't he yell at her
when she was swelling up?
Now he's creased in smiles dandling
his cocoa-butter baby on his knee.
And she feels like wailing,
what's an AB degree compared to that?

She thought she'd try it, too,
stepping out with other men. Sweet Revenge.
But here she is putting up her feet
in stirrups, pink socks, and always
sliding down the table until she's caught
between what she wanted and what she got.
She hopes he gets jumped coming home
from his girlfriend's house. Oh baby,
she'd like him knocked up
a little, maybe bleeding from his ears.

When the nurse looks up and says,
"We're going to treat you,"
she remembers their first date
and the double hot-fudge sundae
they both ate, two spoons, one enormous
plate. He paid. But this shot stings.
Real life, this ain't jimmies on a cloud of cream.

She's gonna turn her life
around and she reads what to watch for
as she laces up her shoes,
shrugs on a jacket, almost happy,
humming a tune she can't quite place.

Arrival

JEANNE LEVASSEUR *Columbia, Connecticut*

Track this on radar: dark-haired girl in heels,
a hundred crew-cut, khakied boys,
barrel down the 10th parallel, a steep landing
toward Long Binh, their last good sleep behind them.
The plane opens to a spitfire of shrapnel,
and the heat, how do I tell you?

The heat opens around you,
as if you dove into a lake
but instead of cool green shafts of water
and a surface you could burst through, chest heaving,
this heat is endless. You know now
you can never go home, you're here
and this heat's all over you.
Even in the first arc of tracer bullets and the dead run
of those blond boys hunched over,
it comes: a whiff of smoke and napalm,
the blossoming mildew. Vietnam
is the hot throat of an orchid,
you must try
and pass through.

The One

JEANNE LEVASSEUR *Columbia, Connecticut*

We built walls nobody could get through,
not even the freshest amputee,
looking up with pain-streaked eyes
as he said, *It's good to see a girl from home.*
You could pretend this was any spring
of ruddy, falling light and the gardenias
just like anesthesia as you eased him back on the stretcher.

In that tangle of blood
was a chance to walk in beauty;
I thought walls were camouflage enough
but one got through for all of us.

The boy I remember
was perfect in his quietness.
His eyes were closed,
sunlight trembled in his lashes.
His hair was straw,
even his fatigues smelled clean,
as if his mother had turned him out to play.
There was nothing wrong with him.
All those others in their bandages and blood,
their bravado . . . I was on my knees,
in a cauldron of orange dust
churned up as choppers huffed above us.
All around me casualties.
He was warm, only fifteen minutes dead,
so perfect,
I could hear his mother calling him.

Shifts

JEANNE LEVASSEUR *Columbia, Connecticut*

I'm two months out of nursing school when Mattie says,
"Come help me turn Mr. Evans."
I go tail-wagging happy to be asked,
like this was a summer dance and we could waltz him
down the dusk-deepened room
to where a soft moon would lay her white feather stole
on the last minutes of this planetary night.

We hook hands in the sour hollows of his arms,
and raise him on the bed, light as all those June bugs
that whir and bump beyond the blind.
He gives a long Ohhhhhh,
all the round breath coming in a hush I should be able to see
but can't yet because I haven't got the Imagination.

Mattie says, "I think he's gone."
Even before she did, I felt my neck hairs prick up
because I'm in two places at once:
here, close up, my hands on his shoulder, one finger
curled inside the open snaps of his johnny, watching Mattie
place her peach frost nails on his pulse, bend her calm neck over
to take his heartbeat. And there, high in the corner of the room,

looking down on us, dust on the doorjamb,
and his table a flat rectangle in a splayed spotlight of roses,
with everything slant, like I'm in the arms of an angel, going
    backwards
and the world's a bright comet streaming out
from this dark ball of a room.

With a long whooosh of breath
I come thudding back.
I've been smacked in the solar plexus,
mewling like any newborn.
And that's how shocking
my first one was.

Miss Smith

PATRICIA MAHER *Brookline, Massachusetts*

I have only good memories
I don't dwell on the Prohibition days
or the raccoon coats
there was a Portuguese fellow and
a yellow Studebaker
but I took care of my father
and stayed a virgin
I'm 98
I'm contented
I'm tired
I'm like a butterfly in a cocoon
when I'm ready to fly
I will

Charlie's Koan

PATRICIA MAHER *Brookline, Massachusetts*

Seventy-four pounds Charlie, you've lost some
I keep my head bowed
my eyes squinting at the
plastic scale.

Charlie steps down carefully
he reassures me
I never was a big man, Patricia.

Anything before I go, Charlie?
Patricia, It's good to be home and
yes, one question.

Is it possible to feel good
before you die?

I look up so quickly
he can tell how much I will miss him
he is smiling.

Why We Wore White

PATRICIA MAHER *Brookline, Massachusetts*

As a young girl
I watched my grandmother dress
for work
creamy belted uniform
pale seamed stockings
chalky clinic shoes
and starched nurse's cap
trimmed with a black velvet ribbon.

My grandmother told me stories
as her hands deftly
fastened her watch
orienting its face
to rest on her pulse
secured her gold pin
squarely over her heart.

I knew she brought babies
into the world
baptized the ones who
wouldn't breathe
promised mothers
that there would be
milk in their breasts
once wrapped a society woman

who had died of a street abortion
and admitted to me
that she had never recovered
from that.

In a photo on her bureau
she stood
with other nurses
they were luminous
hands on hips
broad smiles.
The hope they understood
was the source of my desire
to belong to their
graced sisterhood.

When I became a nurse
we didn't wear white
but learned to recognize it.
The surprise of a pearl
in the shell
the victory of the scar
that has healed
the hope of sails
raised on a mast
the transformation
of plants grown in darkness.

My grandmother's stories
led me to a future
beyond the pale
into work
I had already learned to love.
Stories are the torch we pass
the only way to teach
that mystery of ours —
the capacity
to render light
from the dark.

The Nurse's Job

VENETA MASSON *Washington, D.C.*

. . . with Mom so sick and everyone asking
where's her sister, the nurse . . .

The nurse's job is to make it better
whatever it is
(even a child knows this)
to smooth the forest of furrowed brows
to explain pathologies and pain
to say it will be all right
when it will
and when it won't
to relieve, to be there, to stay.

I have failed at my job.
Even a child knows this.
I offer sporadic intensive care
long-distance counsel
and two thousand miles of excuses.
My absence must smack of
malpractice.

And yet, in the end
there is sanctuary at St. Rose.
As two nurses wedge
between me and her bed
I know I can't distance myself again.
I cling to the rails,
confess that I, too, am a nurse.

You're not a nurse here,
you're her sister
one says, swaddling me
tight in her arms.

I believe she has loved a sister.
I believe that she has known shame.

She does not say
it will be all right
but in her presence
I give in to grief
I begin to let go.
This nurse is doing her job.

La Muerte

VENETA MASSON *Washington, D.C.*

If Muerte comes and sits down beside you,
you are lucky, because Death has chosen
to teach you something.
    Clarissa Pinkola Estes

Old Mother Death sits
down beside me.
Neither cruel nor kind
she does not take, she receives.
We are, all of us, her wards.
Contrary to what you may think
she is in no hurry.
Only humans fret about time.
She squats close to the earth
knees spread wide in a generous lap
and there, mossy shawl drawn
close about her, she waits, shuffling
the letters of her strange alphabet.
I see her fingerpads smudged with ink.
I edge closer.
I am ready to learn.

Negative Conditioning

VENETA MASSON *Washington, D.C.*

At first it was just the needles she hated
    she had bad veins
    and good instincts.

Then she began to hate her doctor
    his face, set like an alarm clock
    his merciless attention to time.

In time, the sight of the fish tank in the waiting room
made her sick
    that queasy medium
    those darting appraisals — piscine and human —
    from the other side of the glass

and the elevator
    sealing her off, in
    before she had pushed the button
    before she was ready

and the short walk from the parking lot
    in spite of the glare
    a fog of premonition

and the drive from home
    no longer behind the wheel
    no longer in control

even leaving the house
    saying goodbye
    shutting the door behind her
    each time
    a rehearsal.

Admission

VENETA MASSON *Washington, D.C.*

Her eyes would blur
so she couldn't see
to fill the syringes.
Often as not
she'd skip the dose
and damn the diabetes.
She'd get groggy
so she'd lose her balance
        and fall —
bound to break a hip one day
land in the hospital
die of complications.
The most complicated things
are simple
in the beginning.
I offer a house call
to check her sugar
and fill the syringes
a week at a time.
I offer to enter
once every week
an uncharted world
not my own.
Enter, do for, exit
        Simple!
Enter, look around, listen
        do for, exit
Enter, wonder
Enter, ask
Enter deeper
Enter

Nurse in Neighborhood
Clinic Disappeared

VENETA MASSON *Washington, D.C.*

It was after we examined the Hispanic woman whose complaint was itching and discomfort in a keloid at the site of a breast biopsy that Eduardo showed me some of his: shiny red burrows, two, three centimeters long, studding his chest like crude tribal markings. "Yes, they itch sometimes," he said, "but there is nothing you can do." That Monday afternoon last summer, the day we saw the lady with the keloid, was the day Eduardo began to tell me his story. I'd heard parts of it from others long before he began volunteering his Mondays at Community Medical Care. Hearing it now from him, in his own language, in snatched moments on a succession of Mondays, I am finally beginning to understand it.

Eduardo is forty, a physician, and married with two children. For the past five years he has lived in the Washington suburbs. Before that, he spent time in Mexico, en route from his own country, El Salvador. He left El Salvador after his release from prison. The imprisonment was only a matter of days, he points out, owing to the fact that the son of a woman who used to sell produce to his mother happened to be well placed in the police department and able to help him. But, he adds, a lot can happen in a short time.

Why was he arrested? He had become interested in working with the poor in a neighborhood not far from his boyhood home. Because he realized that their needs extended beyond the health care he was able to provide, he also taught in a literacy training program and, because life is not all work, began to participate in the social life of the community.

One night some friends, members of a local labor union, arrived at his door with a young man who had been shot. They couldn't take him to the hospital, they said, because the police were looking for him. Eduardo did what he could for the wounded man and the group went on its way. Sometime later the police came for Eduardo. They took him to the station for interrogation.

As they questioned him about the young man and Eduardo's union friends, they smoked. And after each smoke, one of them would lean forward and stub out the cigarette on Eduardo's chest. That was not the worst of it, but it marked him forever. "When I take my children swimming, people stare at me," he says, smiling. "I think they think I have a skin disease." At the lake on the day of our staff picnic, I noticed that Eduardo wore his t-shirt into the water.

Months had passed since my talks with Eduardo began. Then I had a thought I'd never had before. Where it came from I don't know, nor what triggered it. I only know that it seared through my brain like a bullet.

It was lunch time. Eduardo and I were sitting upstairs in the clinic, chatting. He was sipping a Coke. I was peeling an orange. "Eduardo," I asked abruptly, "if this clinic, our little clinic on Ninth Street, were in El Salvador and we were going about our business, just as we are today, would we be considered subversive?" He stopped sipping and looked at me. He nodded his head yes.

Of course we would. We serve the poor. We are affiliated with a church. In addition to giving health care, we sometimes help people get what they are entitled to from the government. It's called advocacy. The Central Americans we see are the same ones Eduardo took care of in El Salvador. And many of our other patients live outside the law.

But *I* am not subversive. Beyond voting, I commit no political acts. I am not even an idealist. I helped to start the clinic because I had a professional interest in primary health care. When I joined Amnesty International, it was in a fit of pique over the ticket I got for disobeying a traffic sign hidden behind a billboard. If this can happen to me on a street in Washington, D.C., I reasoned, think what could happen in a country where there is no protection or recourse under the law!

But is a country like El Salvador really so alien? I have visited there more than once. No, not on a peace mission or fact-finding tour, but accompanying my husband on business trips. What impressed me most each time was the apparent normalcy of daily life. In spite of the fact that this was a country at war with itself, the people I met went to work every day, ate oranges, and drank Coke. Yes, I saw desperately poor people, just like I do in Washington. Sure, the army was everywhere, but so are the police on Ninth Street. When I learned about a resolution put before the American Nurses' Association to protest attacks on Salvadoran nurses working in outlying clinics and hospitals, I felt that American nurses were being given an unbalanced picture of the risks health workers there faced. If nurses disappeared, shouldn't we at least consider the possibility that they were doing more than nursing?

Today, I feel differently. Today, I can imagine myself in a situation where simple advocacy of health care for all could be viewed as a threat to the stability of a political system: I am at the clinic, going about my business, when a man stalks in, flashes a badge and says he wants to speak with me. "What can I do for you?" I ask, taking him into an exam room and shutting the door. "I think you're aware," he says, with no attempt to hide his sarcasm, "that there's a war on law and order in this neighborhood. Mighty dangerous place for folks like you to be working. I'm sure you would claim not to know it, but a few hours ago, a man was seen leaving this clinic — a man suspected of shooting one of our agents two blocks from here yesterday. He got hurt, too, but never showed up in any of the local emergency rooms. Don't you find that interesting?" He pauses, gives me a significant look. "Now, here's my advice," he says. "Move your clinic out of this neighborhood before something bad happens to you. I guarantee that if you stay here, you'll regret it."

What would I do? Would I choose to get his meaning? Would I throw away my investment in this place? Turn my back on these people who may have started out as patients but who have become friends and, some of them, co-workers? I am a nurse. I work for good. I commit no political acts . . . do I?

The Politics of Disease

ELIZABETH KEOUGH MCDONALD *Gallup, New Mexico*

She flew to Canada from Africa — sick. Cough and fever.
When hospitalized, she scared doctors and nurses. Placed
in a negative airflow room reserved for TB patients, she
became what experts couldn't rule out — the Ebola Virus.

The news accused a hemorrhagic killer from another land,
another people. Across the border, aftershocks of
invasion. Under their suits and crinolines, TV reporters
perspired heavily, murmured. "AIDS, now Ebola." The flat

mouthed accusations of coach mingling with first class —
us and them. Others, hat brims turned low over their eyes,
blocked out the gravity. The virus negative, a sigh from
those who know contagion: eenie meenie minie moe.

I've looked out enough windows to know what passes by,
enters.

Bataan Angels

ELIZABETH KEOUGH MCDONALD *Gallup, New Mexico*

The nurses of Bataan and Corregidor were in every sense "at war," side by side with men. The difference was that they carried a battle dressing instead of a gun. They fought, and fought fiercely, to preserve life as everyone around them was bent on taking it. In that light Angels seemed just right.
    Elizabeth M. Norman, *We Band of Angels*

After they survived Bataan,
no small feat in the shadow
of the death march, the military
paraded their anorexic bodies,
bad teeth and unrecovered illnesses
before the families of dead infantrymen —
with hope that a nurse would remember: a
photo would jog memory of how their son
died. Was their father alone when it ended?
Did it take long? Can you tell me? Hours, days,
the nurses sat on wooden chairs, in oppressive halls.
Stood first in formation to salute the flag, listen
to the Star-Spangled Banner, hear the accolades of their
angelic heroism. Wracked with diarrhea, migraines, painful
joints and insomnia, they endured. They, too, had lost
husbands, brothers, fathers in the war. Family members
died while they were captive overseas. Their grief,
the flavor of a circus act, hustled on the back of
a Colonel's promotion. Former Prisoners of War,
the Bataan nurses walked a tightrope — juggled
balls of fire, swallowed the sharpest swords.
They were the greatest show on earth.

A Nurse's Farewell

PAMELA MITCHELL *Saratoga Springs, New York*

1. ## Calling

My hands guided my nurse's
instinct my hands heard
a million voices howling
yipping like wolf pups
longing for sustenance

My hands listened to stories
of fear and uncertainty
my hands listening drew me forward
magnet pulling me along
Perhaps I sensed what lay ahead

2. ## Connection

Longing to connect with another
human rhythm, to feel a beat
singing within my fingertips

We'd nod in agreement
patient and I slowly
we'd search for the song
that held us in gentle synchrony

3. ## Healing

Healing arrived like the flame
I kindled as a child
blowing on a twig singing *Rise up flame!*
like a bone's fracture line
soon strong enough to bear

the body's weight
like the whisper of a child
propelling my hands toward life
begging to touch the next man
or woman or child with those eyes

Oh God those eyes
that fractured my heart again and again

4. Pain

Despite hope I know something
deep within me
healing has not stopped by in a long time
instead fear knocks upon the door
fear like the sucking of marrow

from my bones demanding
I be steadfast when my being
silently shatters like safety glass
writhing bodies lash at me
the words of enraged physicians

the voices of those trusted to administrate
threaten to suspend my work
should I become ill one more time
Fear comes with deep fatigue
like being knocked out

the threat, the deep fatigue
of witnessing unrelenting sorrow
those with inappropriate diagnosis
those not sick enough sent home to die
and this is how we manage our care

5.   Hope

I recall healing's presence
even moments of laughter something
I no longer hear within these walls
except yesterday when laughter slipped in
through the back door by mistake

It's not in my nature as nurse
to let her go

6.   Resolve

I wait and healing does not come
yet I long for it a yearning unlike any
I can recall as adult or child
I must leave I cannot believe it is so

after twenty-five years the price
of being a nurse has become too high
and compassion is on the list of endangered species

Mr. Tims's Morning

MURIEL MURCH *Bolinas, California*

At four A.M., sleep left Mr. Tims with a quiet bow, as if the
dance music had ceased and it was time to move on to a new part-
ner. The two Nembutal sleeping tablets slid out of his blood
stream, through his kidneys and, with an impish glee (Mr. Tims
often thought), into his scant urinary output. The urine gave a
parting, churlish nip and sting to his skin as it leaked and oozed
around the subrapubic catheter that carried its burden into the
grimy bag hanging down from the frame of his hospital bed. Af-
ter his first involuntary grimace, Mr. Tims blinked his eyes open
to the darkness. His was an optimistic nature. As he slowly shifted
his back, guarding in vain against the incoming pain, he also
shifted his mind away from the purpose of the rubber tube that
rose from his abdomen to replace his flaccid penis. It had served
him well enough for seventy years. If he was honest, the burning
pain at the tube's insertion was greater than any caused by a short-
age of prophylactics as an army medic during his war torn youth.
Without any of the fun, he thought ruefully as he shifted once more
in the bed and let out a heavy sigh to cover his breaking wind and
signal the nurse he was awake now.

Sitting at the desk in the center of the small ward, Nurse Ros
Andrew heard him. The lamp arched its light down on the desk,
but she could make out the silhouettes of the men in their beds
curved around her in a wide horseshoe. She bent her head for a last
glance at the page and put down her pen beside the picture of the
eye she was trying to copy and memorize. Nurse Andrew looked
out across the desk and gave a little smile into the darkness. She
knew Mr. Tims could see her and was smiling back, anticipating
her coming to him as a puppy waits for its master, knowing it must
stay in order to receive the attentions that are salvation. Mr. Tims
had no choice but to stay. He was bound to his bed by tubes and
fluids as firmly as if tied by a leather collar and lead. Still he waited,
his eyes twinkling in a face made more sweet by the shininess of
his completely bald head and his cheeks blown round by pred-

nisone. It had been months since the radiation treatments were finished; his remaining tufts of hair had fallen out, never bothering to regrow, a decision the hair seemed to have made all on its own, but one that did not entirely displease Mr. Tims. Sometimes he would raise an arm and pass his chubby hand over his bald pate, each time touching himself in gentle wonder at his smooth, cool head.

Nurse Andrew slipped from behind the desk, the sound of her crisp apron unfolding as she stood up. Her rubber-soled black shoes were lighter and more feminine than regulation uniform, and their purchase had been made on a whim. She picked up her torch and, pointing it downward so as not to wake anyone else, went to Mr. Tims, whose bed was centered directly across from her desk among the semicircle of men who slept as restlessly as nervous camp soldiers gathered for warmth and comfort around the flame of her lamp.

"Hello Mr. Tims."

"Hello nurse." He gave a boyish smile — half apologetic, yet utterly grateful that she had come to him in the night once more.

"Do you need anything?" She asked the question softly, almost vaguely, in a manner that allowed him to be slow in his reply. If he chose to relieve his pain, he could receive an opiate. If he chose to relieve his loneliness, she might stay.

"What time is it?" he asked.

"About four."

"How is the studying going?"

"All right. I still get the brain pathways all wrong. Sister Alexander spent another half hour going over them with me tonight." For twelve dark hours, Sister Alexander circulated through the wards like a calm blue angel watching over the senior student nurses who staffed the wards as well as the patients in their care. From the advantage of eight years more of life, love, and education, and in addition an open heart, she well knew the struggle of these last weeks that led to final exams. Given as much responsibility as staff nurses, senior student nurses knew that this was, in its way, the first and most crucial of their exams. How would each nurse care for her ward *and* focus on her studies? Sister Alexander lingered, as angels do, in Nurse Andrew's mind; however, she drew the conversation back to Mr. Tims.

"Did Mrs. Tims come in this evening?" she asked.

"Oh aye. She was here as usual tonight. She got to hear the carol singers as they came round the ward."

"We heard them too. They were in the hall when we came out of supper and visitors were leaving."

She remembered how she had first heard them — distantly calling into the arched corridor that led from the staff dining room, once the original chapel, into this old red brick tribute to Victorian progress. As she and her friend, Sally, rose from their meal, the high hum became a soprano whisper calling them both until their footsteps quickened and echoed down the stone corridor. The voices of the carolers reeled them toward the great hall. The choristers' voices faded out of "Away in a Manger" and, taking a collective breath, they turned with one heart to welcome the fresh young night nurses with "Good King Wenceslas." After the first verse, the carolers turned toward the stairs and continued singing to the families and friends who were leaving the hospital for the night. A slim young woman dressed in gray with a muted red scarf as her only Christmas ornament and a young boy still in his school uniform moved towards the visitors and rattled little red cans, hesitantly asking for donations. The pence and pounds collected on these nights of caroling would go to the Friends of the Hospital and help stock the patient trolleys wheeled around the wards by the aged men and women who, grateful for some remembered kindness, volunteered on Wednesday and Saturday afternoons.

Ros and Sally had stopped for a moment at the mouth of the corridor during the singing of the "Good King." Ros realized that she had always rather enjoyed this king who knew he was both the protector and the master of his page. He was a human sort of king, she thought to herself. Ros liked to imagine that if you were a thief of necessity caught in his reign, the Good King might give you a good break. As the Good King summoned his page to "mark my footsteps" and "tread thou in them boldly," so did the flow of visitors coming down the stairs freely place coins in the outstretched cans.

The nurses crossed the hall and walked up the stairs, like young salmon swimming against the tide of exiting visitors. They smiled at each other as they heard the clinking of coin into cans.

"Have a good one."

"You too. See you at break?"

"Probably not, I'm going to stay upstairs and study. Mr. Tims usually wakes about that time. I like to be with him now." She did not add that she did not know who would leave the ward first — she to her final exams, or Mr. Tims to his final rest.

"All right. See you in the morning." Sally turned right into Victoria, the women's surgical ward, while Ros turned left and climbed two more stairs, swung under another arch, and entered Edward, the male ophthalmic and neurological ward. The older men on this small ward had mostly undergone eye surgery, while the younger were stricken with an array of neurological conditions that were being watched and treated with floundering efforts by young doctors unable to stop the raging of inflamed neurons tearing through the bodies of the men like horses bolting for home. Occasionally there were patients like Mr. Tims, who ended up here because they didn't fit anywhere else anymore.

It was a quiet, intimate ward, a safe place in which to slip quietly from one world into the next. Ros had entered the ward eight and a half hours ago, well over halfway through the twelve-hour shift.

"Mrs. Tims loves the carols. We used to sing as youngsters in the church, under protest mind, but then we would go out with the Young Farmers group. And it stays with you, you know?" Mr. Tims sighed and looked through the window at the still, black sky, aglow only with the faint orange of the street lamp below. "Aye, it stays with you."

"Are you uncomfortable Mr. Tims? Come forward a moment and let's straighten you up."

As she leaned toward him, he felt her strong, smooth arm reach under his and her other arm circle his back, bending him forward. He smelled her young, fresh body and yearned to touch her skin. She was as precious to him as his granddaughter Sarah. Instead he relaxed, let her punch and puff up his pillows. He braced his arthritic knees and pushed his feeble, sore heels into the bed. Their coordinated efforts moved him up the bed, after which he fell back against the cool sheets and, for an instant, felt the release of comfort.

"Thank you, nurse."

She stood up, paused to relax her back, and looked down on the shiny round man; she wondered how much more he would endure.

"Would you like a cup of tea?"

"That would be nice, if it's no trouble." They went through this exchange as if for the first time, not as the routine they'd settled into over a month ago, their first night together. She left his bedside and walked back toward the kitchen. Passing through the ward, she glanced at the other patients, fifteen men with their eyes closed and their minds — where? Mr. Tims so often appeared to be the only one awake. She wondered if there was an unspoken alliance between the other patients to give him this time. Somewhere she had heard that prisoners on death row let the man who was condemned to die with the rising dawn sing alone all night.

The kitchen was warm. At the beginning of her shift, before she even entered the ward, she'd filled the huge tin kettle and put the flame under it on low. Now it glowed, a blue welcome to her as she entered the kitchen. Through the window she saw Venus shining brightly over the moon, as ethereally round and full as Mr. Tims, she thought.

Nurse Andrew carried the strong, sweet cup of tea back to Mr. Tims. His eyes twinkled as he watched her return to his bedside. His pudgy hands reached out shakily in the dark to grasp both the tea and the moment, stolen with delicious sweetness. He sat forward to allow her to plump up his pillows once more, then slipped back with a sigh of deep contentment. For a moment, all was forgotten as he took a sip.

"Listen nurse, I hear the lorries coming down the hill. It must be a market day today."

"Thursday. You're right." She replied quietly, as she too looked out the window behind his bed to the brow of Hogs Back Road. One by one the yellow street lights led down the road into town.

In the next bed, Reg's eyes blinked open. He turned his head toward the pair. Nurse Andrew was standing close to Mr. Tims's bed, her thigh resting against the turned cuff of his blanket with a lax intimacy, as if, unconsciously, she also drew comfort from his closeness. Reg stirred restlessly, feeling a jealous pang. Nurse Andrew turned her head towards him.

"Good morning Reg."

"Do you think there is a spot in the pot for me?" He asked with a weak grin.

"Of course. Two sugars, right?"

"Thanks love. That'll be lovely."

Nurse Andrew looked down at Mr. Tims and their eyes met, smiling good-bye. She left his bedside and walked through the ward. Now, looking out of the kitchen window across the sink, she could make out the shadowy outline of the cattle market and railway station in the town. Venus lingered in the sky, dimming reluctantly with the rising dawn. She did not switch on the kitchen light.

That Mystique

MADELEINE MYSKO *Parkville, Maryland*

After dinner, when the oven timer beeped at six o'clock, Marcie dried her hands on the dish towel and went to look for her boots.

"I'm going now," she called down the stairs. "I won't be long." While she was extracting the boots from the umbrellas and lacrosse sticks in the closet, the two boys came running down the stairs, one of them jingling the car keys.

"Where are you off to?" Marcie asked. She pulled the curtain aside and looked out. It had stopped snowing hours ago. The road was already dry.

"To the game," the older one said. "Where are you off to?"

"Next door," Marcie said, pulling on her boots. "Remember? To give Charlie his tube feeding. Listen, you two. Be careful on the road. Just because it looks OK, doesn't mean it isn't icy."

"Bye, Mom," the younger one said.

She held the storm door open and watched them go. They took the shortcut across the lawn, both of them in baseball caps, neither of them wearing boots or gloves. She sighed, watching until the car backed out of the driveway and disappeared around the corner.

"I'm going now," she called again, stepping into the stairwell. The girls were out; one baby-sitting, the other at the library. Her husband glanced away from the TV to wave.

And so she was off, at the last minute pulling a red knit hat over her ears, not so much against the cold — she was only crossing the yard — but because she hadn't done a thing with her hair all day. Charlie was the sort of person who took notice.

Hank was the one who had called to ask the favor. Out of the blue some friends had invited him to the symphony, and he wondered if Marcie wouldn't mind coming over at six to give Charlie his tube feeding. There was really nothing to it, he said, as no doubt Marcie was aware, being a nurse herself. He would have everything prepared, and Charlie could tell her what to do. In fact, Charlie could almost take care of it himself, if he just had a little more strength in his hands.

When Hank and Charlie had moved in, some years back, they made it their business to get to know people. They liked to cook and to entertain. They had a big croquet party on their lawn every summer. During the holidays it was an open house. The first year, when Charlie took all the neighbors on a tour of their remodeling, his weakness had been barely perceptible. The handsome walking stick had seemed nothing more than a dapper affectation, handy for pointing out the decorative molding overhead. He led them through the widened doorways, explaining matter-of-factly that certain structural changes had been made in anticipation of the wheelchair he would need—when and if his multiple sclerosis progressed. The emphasis had been on the "if." They had all breezed through on their way to the brand-new patio where Hank was flipping burgers. Who would have paused to picture happy-go-lucky Charlie in a wheelchair? And yet in a matter of a few years, the sure and steady decline had become so familiar that everyone began to take it for granted.

"How's he doing, Hank?" Marcie had asked over the phone. In the winter she didn't see much of the neighbors. Somehow, the news hadn't gotten to her that Charlie required tube feedings now. She was embarrassed that she hadn't called to inquire about him sooner.

"Well, his spirits aren't so good." It seemed Charlie kept aspirating and coming down with pneumonia. He'd been in and out of the hospital three times already since September, and the last time the doctors had insisted on the feeding tube.

"This has been the hardest of all for him — to give up eating," Hank said. "And, of course, his goddamned cigarettes."

"Poor Charlie," Marcie said. She realized then that it had been weeks since she'd noticed the lamp lit on their screened-in porch when she passed by, or since she'd waved to Charlie out there, bundled up in his wheelchair, having his smoke. Right next door, and she had been so caught up with work and the kids and the house that she had completely forgotten about him. "I'm so sorry," she said. "I didn't know you were going through this. I never even sent a card."

"Look, you've got your hands full with that crew of yours, Mar-

cie. Charlie knows that. He keeps an eye on the comings and go-
ings. He gets a kick out of it. 'That's one busy woman over there,'
he says."

"Well, I'm not that busy," Marcie said. "And I'll be glad to
come over. At six o'clock. I'll set the timer so I won't forget."

"Great," Hank said. "Oh, and by the way— don't let him talk
you into a cigarette."

"Well, of course not." Strange that Hank would lay down the
law with her like that. "He doesn't have any cigarettes, does he?"

"No. There aren't any in the house."

"Well then, I don't know how he can talk me into one," Marcie
said, laughing, "because I sure don't have any to offer him."

Marcie was an elementary school nurse. She hadn't seen a tube
feeding since her days in training, so all afternoon she could feel
it approaching— that responsibility of six o'clock. But once she
was outside, following the tracks the boys had made in the snow
and then striking out across the pure white stretch between the
two houses, a certain singleness of purpose took hold of her.
Everything lay cleanly defined in glittering snow— roof line,
bushes, and the little spruces Hank had planted out by the road.
Charlie's window was dark. He would be waiting for her in the
kitchen, on the other side of the house. She paused to look back at
her own house, where too many lights had been left blazing in the
bedrooms upstairs. Then she headed for the porch, where Hank
had said she would find a key in a flowerpot.

"Well, five minutes past six and here she is as promised," Char-
lie said, when Marcie called "hello" and opened the kitchen door.
He was sitting in the wheelchair, facing the counter and a little
TV, on which a reporter was giving an account of a two-alarm
fire. Charlie fumbled with the remote in his lap, and the sound
faded out.

"How've you been, Charlie?" she said, slipping out of her boots,
immediately regretting the question.

He rolled his eyes. "As you can see, I'm in the pink of health.
Even pinker, now that you're here." His speech was noticeably
slower, but the sarcastic edge to it remained.

"Are you going to talk me through this deal?" she said. "Be-
cause I'm not sure I know what I'm doing."

"Absolutely. But first take off your coat and hat. Do you want a
drink? We've got wine, beer, soda."

"No thanks."

"Hank put out some cookies for you, over there on the table." He nodded at a paper plate of sugar cookies, wrapped up in plastic and ready to go. "We have to treat our favorite baby-sitter extra special."

Marcie draped her coat over the back of a kitchen chair and stood there in her stocking feet, smiling at him.

"Don't you want to take your hat off too?" said Charlie.

"Nah. That's OK."

He narrowed his eyes and peered up at the hat as though he could see through it. "Bad hair day?"

"How'd you guess?"

"I have excellent observational skills, my dear. You know that."

Once he had mentioned to her that he'd been studying their deck and couldn't understand why, since she liked to read out there in the mornings, she didn't build herself some sort of lattice overhead. "Vines. It would be attractive, and it would provide you a little shade in the summer." She had liked the idea. In fact, she still pictured it every now and then. But there was never enough time or money for improvements like that at their house.

"Looks like you guys have this down to a system," Marcie said, looking about. The kitchen was spotless — nothing on the entire expanse of the counter but the little TV, a gleaming blender and a gleaming toaster. Next to the sink, on a plain linen tea towel, Hank had lined up the equipment: the barrel, a clamp, extra towels, and a glass pitcher with the feeding in it, already mixed.

"I could do it in my sleep. But the pitcher's a little too heavy for me." It appeared he was as eager as she was to get it over with. He was already working at a button on his shirt.

"Here, let me get that," Marcie said. While she unbuttoned the shirt he slowly lowered his arms. His hands were puffy, white as wax. Under the shirt she found the feeding tube, curled against his white belly.

Charlie took her through the feeding step by step, cautioning her to pinch the tube so it wouldn't dribble on his shirt, reminding her to flush with water. It was done in a matter of minutes. She closed off the tube, buttoned the shirt, and gathered up the equipment in the towel.

"Just leave all that in the sink," Charlie said. "Hank will take care of it when he gets home."

"OK." She filled the pitcher with water and left it standing in the sink.

"When Hank gets home, I'll get my bourbon and water through the tube."

"You're kidding."

"Nope, I'm serious. Can't taste it, of course. But it does relax me, and I can fall asleep. It's not really like having a cocktail. It's more like medicine."

"Well, I'm glad you haven't had to give that up, Charlie," she said, but Charlie wasn't listening. He was slowly moving the wheelchair in the direction of the door, the one leading to the porch.

"Now for a smoke," he said.

"Excuse me?" Marcie said, though she'd heard him perfectly well.

"I said, now for a smoke." This time he looked at her. There wasn't a vestige of humor in his eyes. "I've been waiting for this all day."

"But Hank said you aren't supposed to smoke."

"Hank isn't going to know. This is between you and me. I've got exactly eleven cigarettes left hidden from him. When they're gone, they're gone. But until then, I'm going to have my smoke." He flipped his jacket from the hook behind the door, and it fell into his lap.

She'd been ambushed. Hank might have the upper hand with him, but she was helpless, cornered. "Don't do this to me, Charlie," she said. "You don't want to have to go back in the hospital."

He rolled his eyes and shook his head, as though she'd said something pathetically naïve. "Believe me, my dear," he said slowly, deliberately, "I'll be back in the hospital in no time, but it won't be a lousy little cigarette that puts me there. Now be a sweetheart and help me with my jacket. I don't want to catch my death out there."

"Charlie," she said. She was pleading now, but he was already working his arm into the sleeve.

"I can do this myself, you know. It'll take me a while, but I can do it. It won't be as nice as it would be if you joined me. I thought we might have a pleasant chat out there on the porch, just the two of us, while I have my cigarette."

"Oh come on, Charlie. I'm not going to fall for that."

"What? The pleasant chat? OK. Don't fall for it. But it's the truth. It's part of the whole cigarette thing." He gave her a wry smile. "You know — that mystique."

He was having trouble with the other arm. She couldn't bear to stand there and watch, so she went over and held the sleeve.

"Get the zipper, will you?" he said. "And I'll need my hat and gloves. In the pocket."

She zipped the jacket, and pulled on the hat and the gloves. There was a muffler in his other pocket, a soft blue one. She wrapped it around his neck and tucked it behind his shoulders. "How can I stand by and let you do this?" she said.

"You're not letting me do anything. I can do this without you. All I'm asking for is a little company."

"This is awful for me, Charlie." She couldn't picture him lighting a cigarette by himself — certainly not with gloves on. And what if he caught himself on fire?

"Awful for you maybe, but heaven for me," Charlie said. "I get my cigarette and I get the company of a woman in a charming red hat, and no one's the wiser. The cigarettes are in the front hall closet. There's a seersucker jacket in there. Look in the inside pocket. And bring the lighter. That's in there too."

"I don't think I can do this."

"Sure you can. You worry too much about being a good girl. Look, I know all about cigarettes. They clog up the cilia and leave me vulnerable to infection. You think I'm not vulnerable already? I could choke to death on a goddamned glass of water." He took several slow breaths. The talk seemed to have worn him out. "Come on, Marcie," he said. The sudden plaintiveness in his voice betrayed him then, and she saw that all along he'd been bluffing. If she refused him and went home, no doubt the eleven cigarettes would stay right where they were, stashed in the front hall closet. He wouldn't attempt it without her. He wasn't that stupid. He wasn't that strong.

"Come on," he said again. "I won't even inhale."

She laughed.

"Really. I won't," he said, refusing to laugh with her. "I just want the taste of it in my mouth. A couple puffs. That's all."

"That's all?"

"Yeah. That's all I've got left. A couple puffs."

She went to the hall closet. She found the seersucker jacket, the one he'd worn to the croquet party last summer — Charlie in his crisp suit and straw hat, parked in his wheelchair in the shade. She found the pack of cigarettes and the lighter in the inside pocket. She took them to him and laid them ceremoniously in his lap.

"Good girl," he said.

"I'm going to be worried sick for the next week," she said, pulling on her own coat. "I'm going to be scared to look out my kitchen window, scared I'll see an ambulance in your driveway."

"Relax," Charlie said. "Don't forget your boots."

As she bumped the wheelchair over the door frame and onto the porch he leaned forward, like a kid intent on a joyride, keeping the cigarettes and lighter pressed against his knee.

"Shall I turn on the lamp?" Marcie asked.

"For god's sake, don't do that. Nosy Nancy over there might look out and see us. First thing tomorrow, she'll be on the phone with Hank. Just park me facing away from her windows. We've got light enough."

Apparently the skies had cleared. The snow shone smoky blue around them. Marcie pulled up a lawn chair and sat down beside him. It was cold, but there wasn't any wind.

"Pretty evening," Charlie said, tapping a cigarette from the pack and propping it carefully between his gloved fingers.

"Yes," Marcie said. She took the lighter from his lap. "Allow me."

"Now really, isn't this pleasant?" He held her hand to steady the lighter and leaned into the flame. He drew on the cigarette and blew the smoke to the side. "See," he said, smiling at her, his face so close to hers she could feel his breath, "no inhaling."

They sat in silence. She waited for him to raise the cigarette to his lips again, but he only held it stiffly between his fingers, letting the smoke curl up past his face and over his head. Once he coughed — a small cough, but enough to fill her with terror. After a while he sent her to retrieve an empty soda can — his ashtray, which he told her he'd hidden some months ago behind the firewood stacked by the door. The cigarette burned down, but he did not lift it again, except to occasionally flip the ashes into the can.

"So what shall we talk about?" Marcie said. "I thought that was supposed be part of the mystique."

"Ah yes. The mystique." He looked toward the road. A car went by, the headlights grazing the snow piled along the curb. "Let's see. How about us? Let's talk about us."

"Us?" Marcie said, raising her eyebrows. "OK. What about us?"

"Well, you first. Let's talk about you. How old are you?"

"Gee, Charlie," she said, rearing back. "You're not supposed to ask a lady a question about her age."

"I know. But life's short. There are things I want to know."

"I'm forty-five. How old are you?"

"Forty-seven." He paused a moment, took a shallow puff, and then flicked the ashes into the can. "Did you grow up around here?"

"In the city. Gardenville. I went to St. Anthony's."

"I knew it," he said, shaking his head. "Raised by the good Franciscans. I went to the Little Flower, right down the road from you. Did you ever go to Reed's Candy Store?"

She hadn't thought about Reed's for thirty years, but suddenly she could see the glass cases. Necco Wafers. Bonomo's Turkish Taffy. "We went there all the time. My sister would get the brown Turkish taffy and I'd get the white."

"Fireballs — do you remember the fireballs? I used to buy them by the dozen. I kept one stashed in my jaw at all times. My grandmother was worried I'd burn off my taste buds. But I thought they gave me some kind of power."

Marcie laughed.

"OK," Charlie said. "That takes care of childhood. Now let's talk about love."

"Love? Goodness. You do move fast." She tried to meet his eyes, but he was still looking beyond her, toward the road.

"Remember who you're talking to, my dear." He brought the cigarette to his lips, and squinted through the smoke. "But maybe you'd rather talk about sin, seeing as you probably think you're committing one right now, sneaking around in the dark with the guy next door, giving in to his nasty little vices."

"I do not think that," she said, straightening herself in the lawn chair. He was laughing at her, behind that deadpan face. "All right then, if that's what you want. Love it is. What about love?"

"Well, right now I love you, Marcie." He said it with no more expression than he would have said "Tomorrow is trash day."

She threw her head back and laughed. "You are so outrageous, Charlie," she said. "You do not love me."

"Oh, but I do." He carefully snuffed the cigarette inside the can and let it drop. "I love you and your hat."

"Well, I love you too, Charlie," Marcie said.

"How can you help it?" He flashed a quick smile. "But that's our little secret. This whole mystique thing is our little secret, right?"

"Right."

Later, after she had returned the soda can to its hiding place behind the firewood, after he was settled in the kitchen again, he sent her back outside to give his jacket and muffler a few good shakes in the yard.

"You can't be too careful where Hank's concerned," Charlie said. "He's got this freakish sense of smell."

When she came back in, he held out the cigarettes to her. "Come here and take these," he said. "You keep them for me. Nothing's safe in this house for long."

"OK," she said, and stuffed them in her pocket.

"Don't forget your cookies. Hank will have a fit if you don't take your cookies."

"Thanks."

"And don't give them to those brats of yours. They're for you." He made an attempt at a wink. For the first time Marcie noticed that the muscles in his face seemed to have been affected too. Somehow he appeared to grimace.

"I'll be thinking about you, Charlie," she said.

"Good. I'd like that." He took the remote from the table and turned on the sound. A meteorologist was pointing to a weather map, describing a high pressure system.

"I'll just put the key back where I found it."

"All right. Thanks."

She closed the door firmly behind her. She put the key under the pot. Going across the lawn, she made a new set of tracks in the snow toward her own house, heading this time for the back. When she got to the trashcan, she set the plate of cookies on the driveway, lifted the lid, and dropped the cigarettes in, giving the can a good shake so they'd slip down, out of sight.

"How did it go?" her husband called when she opened the door and stomped her boots on the mat.

"Fine," she called back, and went straight to the kitchen to empty the dishwasher.

Later, when the children came home, first the girls and then the boys, she greeted them gaily from the counter, where she stood making the egg salad to pack in their lunches. Through the window she had a clear view of the house next door. With all the concentration of a fallen woman, she managed to avoid its glance.

I Remember Vietnam

CAROL NACHTRAB *Napoleon, Ohio*

I remember the *Dust Off* pilots who took care of me from San Francisco to my final destination in Nam. They told me where to go and what to do, they carried my luggage, played cards on the plane all night (who could sleep?), and told me what to expect. They were my friends.

I remember being treated with respect, kindness, and protection by every man from every branch of service.

I remember working the night shift, answering the phone to find it was one of the guys calling from the field. He was lonely and wanted to hear the sound of an American female voice.

I remember holding a dying GI, pretending to be his girlfriend, wife, or mother so he wouldn't think he was dying alone.

I remember trying to look my best in the humidity and rain, always wearing perfume. And, as I was changing a dressing, hearing, "You smell so good."

I remember the Navy and Air Force guys who brought the nurses Salem cigarettes and Matuse wine, how brave every man was, how — no matter how wounded they were — they would always ask how their buddy was doing.

I remember Tom.

I remember wondering about all the guys we patched up and sent home. I remember when meeting someone from Ohio was just like meeting a next door neighbor.

I remember how I'd chase the cockroaches out of my bed every night before going to sleep, how we talked about the *real food* in the *real world* — McDonald's and potato chips in a bag.

I remember the beautiful white sand beaches.

I remember when the beauty queens from the USO shows would come into the wards with their designer clothes and perfect hair as we stood by in our fatigues and combat boots, and how a USO girl asked a patient how he felt finally seeing beautiful girls from back home. Looking at us he replied, "No disrespect, ma'am, but my nurses here are the most beautiful women in the world."

I remember when the guys in the hospital couldn't sleep in the beds, because they were used to sleeping on the hard, wet ground.

I remember seeing hundreds of pictures of girlfriends and wives and hoping that when these guys got home these women would understand the times of silence, the times of rage. The nightmares, the tears.

I remember Nam when I hear a helicopter. When I hear the song "Leaving on a Jet Plane."

I remember coming home on leave on a plane that was more than half full of guys returning from Nam. When we went to get our baggage, the airline announced that all military personnel were to wait for their luggage until the paying customers got theirs. I remember crying in the cab all the way to my hotel. The cab driver's wife called me that night to see if I was all right, because they'd lost two sons in Vietnam.

I remember my hometown dedication of a Veterans' Memorial, seeing all the military branches in their dress uniforms, then a small group in faded fatigues standing just as proudly. When I asked if I could stand with them, because I was a Vietnam vet, they embraced me and I became one of them.

I remember attending the reunion in Kokomo and being hugged, kissed, and thanked. It doesn't matter that now I'm older, a few pounds heavier, and have gray hair. I'm loved by those men, no matter what I look like, because I was their nurse.

I remember how the Vietnam vets were the first to welcome home the soldiers from Desert Storm. I remember when my daughter asked me why the country didn't do the same when we vets came from Vietnam.

I will always remember the soldiers who were and always will be the greatest men I've had the honor and privilege to know, to work with, to comfort and care for.

I remember and, if needed, I would go again.

Change of Shift

MIRIAM BRUNING PAYNE *El Paso, Texas*

The day staff hurries in,
washcloth scrubbed
and polyester crisp.
I pass them in the lot,
my outline faded.
The night has absorbed me
like charcoal.

Morning air disperses
night shift nausea.
Ignition exhaust rises,
my car fills with the familiar drone
of *Morning Edition.*
I see mountains
that dam the fog from the sky
and I am reminded of your cut hair
swept against the blue linoleum.

Master of delayed gratification,
I think about yogurt,
my morning-cap toddy,
dream of the restless void,
that delicious sinking.

From the shower I tiptoe
goose-bumped and damp
into our sleeping room.
For a moment I watch the rise
and fall of bedcovers
in the shade-filtered light,
then slide in beside you,
my breasts and stomach

a cool line
against your back,
your special wake-up call,
sweet alarm
for the change of shift.

Car Spotting

CHRISTINE RAHN *Olympia, Washington*

The view from 336, Eddie Oliva's room, swept across the south lawn, past the hospital parking lot, over River Road, through a thicket of red maples, and down an embankment to the mud flats of the Mississippi. I saved his room for last on afternoon rounds. Perched in bed with his nose pressed to the window, Eddie watched the snarled commute on River Road. Horns blared, brakes squealed, and exhaust fumes swirled skyward in the brisk autumn air.

"Hi Sport," I said.

"Hi Alice." The brim of a blue and white baseball cap shaded his eyes. He didn't look up.

"What's happening?"

"A '61 Falcon rear-ended a '59 Caprice." Eddie pointed to the accident three stories below. "Oh boy, this is gonna be a neato traffic jam."

I searched for a thermometer in the pile of comic books, *Car and Driver* magazines, model cars, empty juice glasses, and half-eaten cups of Jell-O on his bedside stand.

"Time to take your temperature, Sport." A whiff of disinfectant stung my nose as I shook down the thermometer.

"There's a '61 Chrysler Imperial," he said. "Cool fins. The cops have a '62 Ford Fairlane. And look over there. A '55 Thunderbird." The reflection in the window glass exaggerated Eddie's features—big brown eyes, snub nose, crooked grin—like a mirror in a funhouse.

"Stay put for five minutes." I slipped the thermometer under his tongue. "Just five minutes." The late afternoon sun streamed into the room. I reached over to close the shade.

Eddie spit the thermometer out and waved me away. "No! Leave it open." He grabbed his Big Chief tablet and a stubby yellow pencil from the drawer of his bedside stand.

"Look! A white '58 Impala. What a beauty. And there's a '53 Olds." He wrote down the years and models in his loopy fourth-grade cursive.

"Don't you ever get tired of cars?"

"Heck no."

"There are so many other things to do, why spend all your time at the window?"

"Because."

"Because why?"

"Just because."

"It wouldn't hurt to do something besides spotting cars once in awhile," I said. "I brought you a book about the Mississippi. It's called *Father of Waters*. Would you like to read it? It has pictures of dams and boats and barges."

Eddie shrugged. "I suppose." He sped through the book, dropped it on the bed, and turned back to the window so fast his baseball cap fell off. The boy in the funhouse mirror vanished.

An old, bald gnome hunched in the bed, eyes ringed with dark shadows, cheeks drained of color. The hairless apparition startled me. I reached over the bed to pat him on the head.

He jerked away. "No mushy stuff." Then he flopped the baseball cap back on, crossed his eyes, pooched his lips and made a fart noise. Eddie was back.

I laughed, relieved at the rescue. "OK, Sport. I have to get to work. See you later — "

" — Alligator."

I waved from the door, but Eddie was back at the window.

At nine o'clock, I stopped by his darkened room. "Do you want the light on?"

"No, I can see better without it. A '64 Rambler just drove into the parking lot."

"You're scheduled for surgery tomorrow, so you can't stay up late tonight. And you can't have a bedtime snack."

"I'm not hungry."

"Do you need anything?" I fluffed his pillows and smoothed his blanket, then pulled the shade.

"I don't think so."

"What else can I do for you?"

"Nothing. I'm fine."

"Don't forget to brush your teeth. And don't open the shade. You have to get some sleep. Tomorrow's a big day; the doctors are going to take out your spleen."

"I know. Miss Perry told me all about it."

"Anything you need before I go?"

"Know what? Dr. Lepmann drives a '57 Mercedes. But I can't tell from here if it's brown or maroon."

The next afternoon, Miss Perry called me to her office for my three-month probation evaluation. She'd been Pediatrics' head nurse for thirty years, ruling the unit with ancient laws — strict visiting hours, rigid dress code, no coddling of patients. The office was a neat, spare room with nothing personal on the walls except her 1925 diploma from Sacred Heart Hospital School of Nursing.

The other probationers had warned me she could be picky, but I wasn't worried.

"You wanted to see me?"

She wore a nurse's cap starched into three stiff peaks like a crown. "Miss Eastwood, you appear to have mastered the duties of evening charge nurse quickly and well. I've received compliments on your work from Dr. Lepmann, your co-workers, and parents of the children. You're very efficient."

I smiled politely. I knew efficiency was important to Miss Perry.

"However," she said, "you have one area in need of improvement."

I had no idea what it could be. I leaned forward in my chair.

"You become too personally involved with the patients. I'm speaking of Eddie Oliva. Given his circumstances, I'm sure you mean well, but it's not wise to become emotionally involved. It can create a dilemma."

"A dilemma?"

"Nurses must make decisions based on objective data. Becoming too attached can cloud professional judgment."

I wasn't the one with clouded judgment. She was so old-fashioned. Out of date for the '60s. We learned in nursing school that emotional needs and physical needs were equally important. Especially for pediatric patients. Eddie's mother rarely visited. He needed me.

Miss Perry stood up. "We need to maintain emotional distance for our sake as well as the patients'. I want you to re-examine your relationship with Eddie and we'll talk again in two weeks."

A hard, mid-November freeze fogged Eddie's window.

"Wipe it off so I can see," he said.

He tried to kneel, but the effort tired him. I propped him up with pillows like a little prince on a throne. He was getting weaker. His leukemia had not responded to the splenectomy, nor to a course of radiation, nor to another round of chemotherapy.

Dr. Lepmann stayed late pouring through the *Annals of Pediatrics* and consulting with the oncologist. At nine o'clock, he looked up from his pile of books on the desk in the nurses' station. A thumb print on the lens of his glasses obscured his left eye, his brown hair frizzed like a bad home permanent, and he'd misbuttoned his rumpled doctor's coat.

"Miss Eastwood, call Mrs. Oliva. She should be here."

"I've already called her." I didn't mean to sound smug, but I'd made a game of trying to read Dr. Lepmann's mind, anticipating medication orders, second-guessing procedures, predicting treatment choices. If I guessed right, I added a point to my score. I'd accumulated fifty so far. Not bad for a rookie.

"She doesn't have a home phone," I said. "I had to call her at work. She has problems getting time off, and her daycare doesn't take children overnight."

Dr. Lepmann cleaned his glasses with the hem of his lab coat. "Then call Mrs. Jay. Tell Social Services to do something."

"I talked to Mrs. Jay this afternoon." Fifty-one. "She sent a voucher for the bus trip. Mrs. Oliva has to change buses in Duluth." I turned around, but Dr. Lepmann was nowhere in sight. The chief resident was famous for quick getaways. He often left staff looking as if we were talking to ourselves.

I attached the medicine cabinet keys to my belt, picked up the clipboard, and started on evening rounds. This time Eddie was my first stop. He'd been moved to room 302 next to the nurses' station, reserved for our sickest patients. His eyelids were swollen the size of birds' eggs, yellow matter crusted his lashes, and blood oozed from his split lips. He lurched forward, grabbed the emesis basin and retched. I patted his shoulder until he leaned back into his pillows. "I have to finish rounds," I said. "I'll come back later."

He struggled to sit up. "Where's my tablet?"

"You don't need your tablet. You need rest."

"No, I want it."

"You can hardly see."

"I want it."

I took Big Chief from the drawer. "Here, Eddie."

He clutched the tablet to his chest as if it contained sacred text.

The next afternoon, Mrs. Jay showed up wearing her usual navy blue blazer and sturdy oxfords. She carried a worn leather briefcase. She looked around the nurses' station and, spying no medical staff, plopped into the padded chair usually reserved for doctors.

"Did you call me?" she said.

"Yes," I said. "Is Mrs. Oliva coming to see Eddie?"

"I don't know. I sent her a bus voucher. I offered to pick her up. She's got four other kids, you know, and no husband, no one to help. Her parents can't get out of Cuba since Castro took over."

"But it's her son."

"She says she can't afford to come more than once a month because she's trying to save money to move back to Florida. I think it's a good idea. She has relatives there." Mrs. Jay opened her briefcase, took out a bag of corn candy and tore it open with her teeth.

"Move Eddie to Florida?" I dropped my stethoscope. When I stooped to pick it up, my knees buckled. I felt lightheaded.

"Not until he's in remission, of course." She popped a handful of kernels into her mouth.

Snow fell the day after Thanksgiving. The lawn, the parking lot, the road, the mud flats — everything turned white except the Mississippi. The river, a sullen gray, relentlessly coursed its way south. At three in the afternoon, Mrs. Jay showed up at Eddie's door. "Look who's here." She led a petite, black-haired woman into the room.

The woman carried an Army parka over one arm and held a canvas duffel bag in the other.

"Eddie?"

"Mama!"

"Eddie!" She dropped the coat and bag, ran to the bed and kissed Eddie all over his face. "My little man. My biggest boy. I've missed you so much."

Splotches of red lipstick smeared his cheeks. The baseball cap fell off. He jumped off the bed, retrieved the cap and flopped it sideways on his head. His goofy grin made us laugh. Then we cried. Mrs. Oliva blew her nose. Eddie grabbed her hand and led her on a tour of his room, showing off his possessions like a proud purchaser after a shopping spree.

"Look at my model cars," he said. "The Chevy's my favorite. I have books, too. Alice gave me this book about the river. She gave me that World Series pennant on the wall, too." He grabbed the brim of his baseball cap. "Isn't this a neat cap? A real Minnesota Twins player gave it to me. In person. He said he was from Cuba too, and he has our last name!"

"You're my lucky boy." She hugged him again.

"How long will you be visiting?" I asked.

"I have to go back on the midnight bus."

"Tonight?" I said. "That's not long enough."

"I don't have a place to stay."

"Eddie doesn't have a roommate," I said. "You can sleep on the empty bed."

Eddie pulled on his mother's sleeve. "Please. Please."

"Isn't that against the rules?" Mrs. Oliva said.

"We can bend the rules." I bit my tongue. How would I keep Miss Perry from finding out?

"I'll call my neighbor. Maybe she can keep the kids an extra night."

"You can use the phone in the nurses' station."

The neighbor agreed. Eddie whooped for joy. When I checked at seven o'clock, he and his mother were reading the river book. A half hour later, they played *Go Fish* and *Clue*, then at eight they worked a picture puzzle. At eight-thirty, she wheeled Eddie to the lounge to watch TV. At nine, she fed him strawberry Jell-O and bananas, more food than he'd eaten in days. They whispered late into the night. On midnight rounds, I found them in Eddie's bed with their arms wrapped around each other, sound asleep, as if they had no cares in the world.

I walked home, head down against the cold wind. Except for an occasional flash of headlights, River Road was dark. I thought about Eddie's mother. She wasn't the one who'd made sure he had clean pajamas, a warm blanket, a book to read. She wasn't the one who'd coaxed him to eat. Who'd cleaned his vomit. Who'd washed his mouth and treated his sores. Or tucked him in every night for the last three months.

The cold had numbed my hands and feet by the time I reached home. I fumbled for the key. Inside the chilly apartment, I turned up the thermostat, pulled a blanket over my shoulders, and waited in the kitchen for tea water to boil. I pictured Eddie and his mother in bed with their arms around each other. When she was there, he acted fine, hardly sick at all.

The water bubbled. Two cups of hot chamomile made me drowsy. I took an extra blanket from the closet and went to bed, but sleep didn't free me from the vision of Eddie and Mrs. Oliva. So what if she rarely visited? She was the one he smiled for, rallied for, paid attention to. She was the one he needed. Miss Perry was right. It was wrong to get attached to Eddie. He didn't need me.

The next afternoon, Mrs. Jay waited for Mrs. Oliva to pack her duffel bag.

"Can't you stay?" I asked.

"I want to," Mrs. Oliva said, "but I have to pick up my kids and get back to work. I don't want to lose my job. I'll come back soon, I promise." She stroked Eddie's cheek. "You'll be all right, won't you my little man, my biggest boy?"

Eddie put his arms around her neck and held on.

She kissed him, undid his embrace, and backed away.

"We'd better go," Mrs. Jay said. "We don't want to miss the bus."

After his mother left, Eddie slid under the covers.

"Would you like me to rub your back?" I said.

He shook his head.

"Would you like some Jell-O?"

He turned toward the window. The cars on River Road glittered in the winter sun like a string of holiday lights.

"Where's my tablet?" he whispered.

"I thought you gave up cars. You didn't watch them at all when your mother was here."

"Where's my tablet?"

I dug it out of the drawer.

"Give it to me." Eddie leaned toward the window. "I think I see a '49 Hudson Hornet. Do you see it?"

"Yes, I see it. I see all your cars." I leafed through his tablet, through pages and pages of years and models.

"Alice?" The nurse's aide called from the door. "Miss Perry wants to see you."

Miss Perry sat at her desk, hands folded like a grammar school teacher's. "You know it's against the rules to allow visitors to stay all night, Miss Eastwood. And you shouldn't bring Eddie presents."

"Yes, but his mother —"

"It's time we discussed your personal involvement with patients again. If you can't maintain professional distance, I'll have to transfer you. Maybe to a unit where getting attached to patients isn't as easy. Like the OR."

A transfer? She didn't understand. I hated surgery. Pediatrics was the only place I'd ever wanted to work. I loved the patients. Not just Eddie. All of them.

"Please give me another chance," I said. "I'll be professional. I promise."

Miss Perry agreed to extend my probation provided I treated Eddie no differently than I did the other patients. She would be watching. On rounds, I carefully paid attention to every child, reviewed every chart and talked with every parent. I studiously copied orders, stocked the medication cabinet, and double-checked vital signs. I was so busy, I earned no game points second-guessing Dr. Lepmann.

But as the evening wore on, I found excuses to stop in Eddie's room.

"Do you want a glass of apple juice?"

Eddie shook his head. "You already gave me one."

A few days before Christmas, Eddie's condition became acute. He slipped in and out of consciousness. He didn't know our names or what day it was. Dr. Lepmann ordered nasal oxygen, transfusions of plasma and packed cells, and IV vincristine, prednisone, and methotrexate. On December 21, around midnight, Dr. Lepmann sank into the padded chair in the nurses' station, took off his glasses, and rubbed the bridge of his nose. He'd been up since five in the morning.

"There's nothing more to do," he said, "but wait and see."

When I arrived the next afternoon, the ward clerk was stringing red and green garlands in the nurses' station, a volunteer was decorating a plastic Christmas tree in the lounge, and the day shift nurses were busily discharging the ambulatory patients for the holiday. Only the sickest children remained.

I phoned Mrs. Oliva at the restaurant. "Please come. Eddie's very sick." She said maybe she'd come the day after Christmas. I turned the phone over to Dr. Lepmann. "You try."

"Eddie's leukemia doesn't seem to be going into remission this time," Dr. Lepmann said. "You need to be here." He listened for a moment, then resumed his pleas. Finally he hung up. "She's coming as soon as she finds a sitter. Then she'll catch the bus. She wants us to take care of her little man until she gets here."

On the twenty-third, Dr. Lepmann downgraded Eddie's condition to critical and wrote a no-code order.

My shift ended at midnight. I put my coat on, walked to the elevator, and stood in front of the doors. Then I walked back to 302 and looked in. Eddie was asleep. I wanted to stay. I took my coat off. But if Miss Perry found out, she'd transfer me. I put my coat back on, walked back to the elevator and pushed the button. I waited. I glanced at the floor indicator. Stuck on eleven. I looked to see if it would go up or down. It went up. I walked back to Eddie's room. I could sneak one last peek before the elevator made it to the third floor.

Eddie'd fallen asleep wearing his baseball cap. The brim shaded his eyes, deepening the dark circles under his lower lids. His breathing was shallow and irregular. I stroked his cheek. He felt hot. "No mushy stuff," I whispered. I sat on the chair and leaned my head against the bedpost.

The night nurse poked me. "Alice?"

"What time is it?" I blinked awake and stood up. "Is Mrs. Oliva here?"

"Not yet. It's one-thirty. Why don't you go home?"

My hands felt sticky and sweat soaked my uniform. I was still wearing my wool coat. "I'll stay with Eddie until she comes." I took the coat off and hung it over the chair.

"We're short-staffed tonight, so it's OK with me, but what will Perry say?"

"She'll never know. I'll leave before she gets here."

Eddie burned with fever. I sponged him with cold washcloths. He strained to open his eyes and sometimes he recognized me, but most of the night he didn't respond. We both dozed on and off.

At six in the morning, his eyelids fluttered and his right eye opened a crack. He managed a weak grimace. His right hand pawed the air. I moved to the edge of the bed and took him in my arms. He was cool to the touch and smelled like sour milk. I clasped his hand. His fingers curled around mine like a newborn's.

About an hour later, he quit breathing. His grip loosened. I held him for a few more minutes, then, stiff from sitting so long on the edge of bed, I slowly stood up, laid him on the bed and pushed the call button.

Miss Perry answered. Damn.

"Eddie just died," I said.

"I'll get Dr. Lepmann."

I hardly recognized the chief resident. He wore a pressed doctor's coat, Brylcreem slicked his hair into place, and his glasses were spotless. He examined Eddie without disturbing the baseball cap and pronounced him dead.

"Here's the death certificate," I said. "Ready for your signature."

"I swear you can read my mind, Miss Eastwood." He scribbled his name on the form.

I didn't count the point. The game no longer mattered.

"Back to work," he said. "Patients are waiting."

I thought about starting the morgue procedure, but I couldn't do it. The aide would have to. I'd just wait for her, then I'd go. I stood at Eddie's window and watched the sun rise, a hazy pink light on the horizon beyond the frozen mud flats of the Mississippi.

Miss Perry tapped me on the shoulder. I hadn't heard her come in. Without a word, she handed me the morgue pack. She expected me to prepare Eddie's body. I didn't want to do it. She was going to transfer me anyway. I shook my head, but she laid the morgue pack on the foot of the bed and left.

I waited for the aide to arrive. Five minutes passed — it seemed like twenty-five — still no aide. I looked up and down the hallway. The unit was silent. Most of the patients had been discharged for Christmas. Maybe no aides were on duty. I would have to take care of Eddie myself.

I opened the morgue pack. My hands trembled as I filled a basin with warm water, took his cap off and washed his bald head. A few wispy curls clung to his temples. I wiped the matter from his eyes, pulled the IV needle from his arm, cleaned his sores, and washed his body. When he was ready, I wrapped him in the paper shroud and called the morgue.

The orderly arrived, lifted Eddie onto the stretcher, and wheeled him to the elevator, the squeaky wheels echoing in the deserted hall. I sorted his possessions — the Twins cap, the flannel bathrobe, his model cars, the *Giant Picture Book of Transportation*, a stack of *Car and Driver* magazines, and his Big Chief tablet. I filled two brown paper bags to go home with his body. I kept two things I'd given him — *Father of Waters* for my nephew and the World Series pennant for the passionate Twins fan with a heart condition in room 312.

The housekeeper arrived with her bucket, mop, and a pile of clean linens to ready the room for the next patient. I stayed to help. When we finished, I headed down the hall. The day shift nurse stopped me in front of the nurses' station. "Wait, Miss Eastwood. Miss Perry wants to see you."

Damn again. I kept going. I knew what she had to say. But I didn't walk fast enough. She charged out of her office, white cap flapping, and headed me off at the elevator.

I pushed the button, the doors opened.

"Wait." Miss Perry stepped between the doors and held them open. "I want to thank you for staying with Eddie. Our children should not die alone."

The doors shuddered, but she held firm, arms and legs outstretched like a snow angel.

"Take an extra day off," she said. "Come back after the holiday." She stepped back and allowed the doors to close.

The trip down the elevator through the lobby to the front door was a blur. Poinsettias and pine wreaths blended together in a whirl of red and green. People called "Merry Christmas" to each other. I felt as if I were watching a movie. Nothing in the scene applied to me. I was numb. I wondered how I was going to make it home.

But when I stepped outside, my senses revived. The rising sun glinted off the icy surface of the Mississippi in shades of pink and yellow. Along the river bank, thickets of barren maples cast spiny shadows on the fresh snow. On River Road, a fender bender had turned the morning commute into a spectacular traffic jam. A crowd of rubberneckers had gathered at the intersection.

I pointed to the crumpled automobiles. "That's a '61 Chevy Bel Air and a '62 Ford Mustang. And a '59 Studebaker. And a '60 Pinto."

Cars stretched around a bend in the road as far as I could see. I knew the year and model of every one.

Pre-op

GERI ROSENZWEIG *Ossining, New York*

Smocked in blue, nurses flock
to my body as the snows
of April feather the bud.
Wildflowers of childhood
allergies blossom again
in the margins of charts.
Petals of blood flutter
from a vine tapped
in my right arm.
Measuring a scar bedded
like a briar in my side,
they question why earth
took father too soon,
why mother still loiters on the road.
The song of my heart arrives
like music piped from a distant hill.
Snow glazes the sill
when they leave me,
a plot of ground swept clean
for the hooded stranger
who comes with a keen knife
to prune the dark root
sprouting on my kidney.
Thatched in linen
I'm a crocus sleeping
beneath the snow:

O body,
in all the tattered gardens
it is spring.

Covert of Zero

GERI ROSENZWEIG *Ossining, New York*

1.

By the time I got there she had thrown
off the halter of oxygen, left generations
of snapshots taped to the wall.

Hair combed back the way she liked it,
face smooth except for the bruise
of a thumb mark over her right eyebrow,

she left the list of her days in the priest's
pocket, the wheel of her wedding
ring in the palm of her son's hand.

2.

Take a detour into the province
of absence near water flowing
deep with its own intentions.

She's there, among wing beats,
wafer of the end melting on her tongue.
Poised in the half light, tense

as a bird in the covert of zero,
she senses migration in the keys
and hooks of her spine, in the rattle

of weeds along the margins.
Nothing will flush her into my sights,
her name rustling against

the roof of my mouth, nor the red
pleated skirt she left draped
on the end of the bed.

What Was Left of Summer

GERI ROSENZWEIG *Ossining, New York*

With nothing in my mouth but the salt of old times,
I came to the ringing down of the leaves,
to the flower nodding its russet head in the window
box of my mother's last window.
Her voice lifted dry as weeds in the driveway
of the nursing home, minnows of light wavered
on her forehead, a hammer coughed in the garden
as workmen raised a trellised gazebo
in what was left of summer. To make time pass
between us, we composed a past in which
neither recognized the other. I held her hands
from plucking the sheets, offered the charity of water
from a plastic cup, promised to come again,
before it's too late, before they throw out
her cracked slipper and weather turns cold, before
strangers inherit her front door and she becomes
a hallway of regret I walk through at dusk, my face
stunned as a child's at how suddenly the story ends.

What Nurses Do on Their Day Off

JO-ANNE ROWLEY *Denver, Colorado*

A friend said
a day off is just that —
a day off.
No cooking.
No cleaning.
No shopping.
No laundry.
No chores.

I don't usually take advice,
but this sounded good,
so I took the day off,
laid around in the yard
fanning through old magazines.
I teased the cat with a twig
and hummed an old Elvis tune.

The sun was warm on my face
when it occurred to me
there was nothing for dinner,
clothes were heaped on the floor,
the cat's box was full,
the car needed gas.

I thought about my friend.
That phony.
I never liked her much anyway.

A Pediatric Nurse over Time

JUDY SCHAEFER *Harrisburg, Pennsylvania*

Now finally — time
Seeing my first grandson
I am reminded
of someone I know
Miracles are small
One
at-a-time
Two
Three
Four
Five
Six
Seven eight
Nine
Ten fingers
Ten pink toes
Soft eyelashes
Paper fingernails
Window pane eyelids
Moist smell of baby dew
First vision of an angel
      (After all those bittersweet years
      spent with other people's children
      My own with a latch key in her pocket)
Time — now finally
Welcome for a second grandson
Your big brother and I walked
downtown for ice cream
chocolate chip mint
polite, seated at a table
while your mommy labored
Along the way we found
feathers, stones

and prickly "porky-cones"
one dime
and a friendly gray tiger
kitten
napping on a sun-filled
New York village spring day
Your Dad relieved and your
Mommy needing rest
A cell phone call to Opa
We welcomed you
Your big brother offered animal cookies

Long Distance Call

JUDY SCHAEFER *Harrisburg, Pennsylvania*

*In gratitude to friends in Ireland, and especially Tralee, who extended
extraordinary kindness to my husband and me on September 11, 2001*

Learned the value Tuesday
of words
Peace-in-chaos of having said them
World Trade Center hit
Both towers down
White House evacuated
Pentagon fire, stock exchange shut
Plane down near home, dead
American airports-airspace closed
Sipped Guinness, watched TV
hungry for news, our children

All the lines to New York
    Busy
        Search, IV
            Declaring my nursehood to Aer Lingus

(Mentally assessing the war worthiness of my
                triage skills)
            Please, get me home, get me home
        Rescue, IV
    Busy
All the lines to New York

Famished for words, our children
counted our money, scoured TV
Aliens in a country we held dear
Green-white-orange at half mast
Ireland soft and gauzy around us
we wandered, beggars-for-word, in Tralee
Held hands when we crossed the street
Learned the value Wednesday
of words
spoken before we left the States
Finally renewed in a long distance call

A Bridge

JUDY SCHAEFER *Harrisburg, Pennsylvania*

Then came the day that he understood what language was —
a bridge between the flesh and the spirit.
    Dermot Healy, *A Goat's Song*

Cat cries, dog barks; on a hill a starling
starts to descend into this re-moat valley
We shoo him away for lack of prettiness
We call the bluebird; build houses in the field
and in the crisp clear fence rows for him
We pull damp twigs, pieces of rope, from boxes
and clean them for the bluebird each season

The bluebird shy and easily frightened
some say they kill the sparrow for intrusion
To protect the bluebird, is what they say
      I have not killed for the word, yet
      but strongly suspect that I could
I would; would that is, if I had to —
to keep the pulsing bridge afloat

Astronomy and Nursing

JUDY SCHAEFER *Harrisburg, Pennsylvania*

*Cautiously he tested the bars of his cage and found them
not so rigid as they had been before.*
  John Banville, *Dr. Copernicus*

We passed the cage, watched the minimal
flight, bright birds, gold plumage
Black aviary eye watched back
Pacing, walking, dulled by maps
detours and protocol
Green birds fed from routine troughs

Drapery of softest white covered the bars
    A tethered tapestry of sleep
Cover of day, silk ceiling of the night
for eaters of seed and occasional worm
By light curtain dropped, the bird was free
    A feathered peace was marked
for those passing in the green murky dark

The urn internal carries light
in eyes and face and skin
Trust the light, follow the beam

Open the gilded door
with your feathered wing
with your own laser key

Terminal Nurse: Reflections on New Millennium Nursing

JUDY SCHAEFER *Harrisburg, Pennsylvania*

I have seen the enemy
The enemy looks a lot like me
Telecommute from hospital and home
Computer tops lapping
Umbilical phones, palm pilots and pagers
Clinical power point presentations   ʹ
      Deadline
      Deadline
      Panic
Computer and e-mail not working
Virus? Worm? Skill? Skill?
Frozen screens, none synchronizing
      Help
Help desk a phone call away
and the ease of waiting for hours
Waiting for the upgrade
      I'm losing you . . . I'm losing you
Mobile phone tapping
Working longer, working more
      Help
E-charts, e-mail and e-deadlines
E-reprimands, e-ugly and e-nice
On-line, down-line, up-line
      Down time
      Second hand stress
      Virtual and real

O Yeats speak to me — please
I will click now; click *and go to Innisfree*
Walk past the parsley and the arborvitae
Talk to the young mother next door
I hear — I hear baby cries of un-napping
— session disconnected —

Eurycleia

JUDY SCHAEFER *Harrisburg, Pennsylvania*

Trek back home with the scars
Some healed and some healing
Some scars identify us
Some scars reveal us
Some scars disguise us
The good nurse — the old nurse
moves the bath water with her hands
        slowly she
        lifts her eyes
The return is now complete
The wandering one is home
Feet bathed and hair combed
clothing fresh and rebelted
Traveling dust sifted with memories
pushed over the sill of cobble stone,
Green upon the handle of the broom
Proud of some scars
Some identify and reveal — some disguise

Home Visits

PAULA SERGI *Fond du Lac, Wisconsin*

No wonder I paused at their doorsteps,
measuring the distance between us:
my shining young skin, my white teeth, white shoes,
my crisp jacket, new job, fresh breath.
Before the knock I'd hesitate, checking their charts
for the wound from where the pressure of time
had worn holes in their skins.

Most were near the end of their unpeeling,
shedding layers of memory and money.
On the other side of their doors, the acrid
ammonia of urine melted in their bedding,
their trousers and stockings. Drainage-soaked
gauzes trailed behind as they shuffled
to answer the bell.

I wrote *care plans* directing my visits,
mapping the way those wounds would heal,
from the outside in, and listed what I'd use
to fill them: ointments and creams,
plastic sheets like skin itself glued over
their oozing gaps. Orange-colored scrubs
or vinegar. Even sugar sprinkled on like faith.

With my little healer's tools I listened to the pressure
of blood against their vessels as their corpuscles tried
to escape. Catheters drained their amber urine
and plugged up and had to be plumbed. Urine bags
hung like handbags over walkers or bed rails.
I poured their pills into plastic cups, marking
time on calendars big as their kitchen tables.

But I was distracted: the corners of their homes,
the cobwebs and cuckoo clocks, veneer end tables,

scratched woodwork, what the windowsill
figurines could say. Sometimes I'd hear about
lovely mothers, the children that they never saw again.
And when the hour was up, I'd shout
my instructions and leave.

It's not that I didn't want to touch them.
We had no idea, back then, about age
passing itself on. It's taken years
for me to recognize a skin that won't
bounce back, a stuttered gait on icy walks,
elusive words that hide behind
the floaters in my eyes. Once in a while

I'd see it when I washed their bony backs,
a used-up body about to life off
with scapular wings. The glitter of dust motes
above their bird-like heads as they sat
by their windows watching me coming
and going, still lives of another kind. Above
little cloud-tufts of hair, haloes for the almost dead.

On Switching from Nursing to English

PAULA SERGI *Fond du Lac, Wisconsin*

Losing the white nursing shoes was easy —
they made my size eights go on forever,
boats that said too much,
defied the fashion rules for Labor Day, and Easter.
Dumping the uniform was good for self-identity.
I don't miss the contact with bodily fluids,
and I feel nauseous less frequently in class.

But, as any student of the English language will say,
the problem is the spelling.

Grimm did not explain the sudden shift from *b* to *v*
and I write *bowel* all the time.
Come to think of it, no bowel shift allows for what happens
to the *e* from *pleural* and I think *pleurisy, effusion,*

a plethora of problems with the lung, over and over, to indicate
more than just once. Confusion reigns longer
than William, and I attribute it
to the influence of French.
These days I'm better dressed, but
where am I headed with a longer,
misspelled resumé?

Long-Term Companion

JESSICA SHRADER *Wylie, Texas*

Not a word in honor of the long-term companion,
Of the one who kept track of the pills, sat up nights,
Fixed the eggs if eggs were what he promised he would eat.
Ignored in life and hidden in death; the hypocrisy must burn
  your soul.
But I know who you are and what you did and who you were to
  him.
You did not bear his children.
You did not dance with him at the prom.
But you escorted him through his last breath; you opened the
  door
and granted him permission to leave when everyone else insisted
  he stay.
You may not have been the love of his life.
More important, you were the love of his death.

Girl

KELLY SIEVERS *Portland, Oregon*

The summer I was sixteen, I steadied myself on new crepe-soled shoes and pulled a muslin curtain around the bed of Adele Mueller, my first real patient. One curtain away, Florene, another aide, older than me by four years, sang Baby, baby, where did our love go? as she swept linen from a bed. Florene thought she sang like Diana Ross. I thought she was as beautiful as Diana Ross.

Bath time, I told Mrs. Mueller, and although, because of two strokes, she never responded to me, I talked to her. I'm going to cover you with this bath towel. This is warm water. I tightened the wrap of my washcloth and tested it on her arm. I exposed one leg, slid down its arc into slots between her toes. Sister Leota's medicine cart squeaked down the hall as I rinsed the washcloth in clean water. I lathered Mrs. Mueller's belly last, filling the air between us with the sharp smell of Dial. Then, in silence, I moved toward her hidden folds, exposing an awkward, musty smell.

Florene showed me how to pull Mrs. Mueller's hip and shoulder toward us. We held her heavy body; she made no sound. Beneath my hand her shoulder sighed; I patted it as Florene said, "It's all right Adele." Johnnie Mae, Florene's friend, washed and rubbed Mrs. Mueller's back. Johnnie Mae was older than us, her skin darker than Florene's creamy brown, her washcloth's strokes more deliberate than ours. Her eyebrows were penciled black and they arched high when she asked, "Have you heard about Gloria?"

Gloria was the night nurse whose eye I had seen black and blue and whose hair escaped in lonely strands beneath her cap. Johnnie Mae leaned across Mrs. Mueller's hips and said, "She called in sick again. She lost the baby because he kicked her." I gasped and shifted my hands.

Mrs. Mueller's skin moved beneath my hold, loose from her bones as if no longer part of her. Florene shook her head, "I just don't know. I just don't know what we can do."

"Over we go Adele." Johnnie Mae turned our patient toward

us, and she and Florene started to talk about men. Gloria's husband was a sweet talker and a sorry, mean drunk. Someone's man had a heart condition and was in a hospital in Chicago. Should they go see him? Florene's Jimmy had a new job. Then Johnnie Mae leaned close and whispered something to Florene about a new man named William, who was too big for her. I felt my face and neck leap red. Florene flashed a look-who's-here-listening glance from Johnnie Mae to me. She motioned for me to pull the sheet across the bed; I got busy straightening the sheet. When I looked up Johnnie Mae asked me, "You have a boyfriend?"

We propped Mrs. Mueller's paralyzed arm on a pillow and I started to comb her hair. I was silent too long, sifting for an answer, yes and no, thinking about William, about what I knew and didn't know. I thought about my sister's boyfriend, Tim Anders, who rode the bus with us and draped his arm around her at James Bond movies. My legs felt hot and itched beneath thick white stockings.

Florene smoothed the linens, slid her hand to mine. "Girl," she told me laughing, "you have a lot to learn."

Florene had a boyfriend who picked her up every day after work in a blue Buick. When he leaned across the front seat to open the door for her, I saw his arm firm with muscles, his smile true. Before she left work each day, Florene fussed with her hair, brushed her uniform, and glossed her lips with deep pink lipstick. Her skinny hips swayed when she walked to the car, just like they did when she carried breakfast trays down the hallway. She bounced a little, too, and I liked to follow her. Johnnie Mae balanced a tray with one hand and swung her hips slow, like she intended to be late for wherever she was headed. My hips were in the business of walking; I held a tray with both hands, straight out in front of me, and moved forward.

We left Mrs. Mueller propped on pillows and clean. When we delivered lunch trays, I noticed her white forehead close to the bed rail, her eyes open. Next job, I knew, would be turning Mrs. Mueller. In the men's ward, I touched men gently on shoulders to waken them from naps, rolled up heads of beds, opened milk cartons, poured coffee. "You leave her alone now," Florene fired toward any man who teased his way toward me.

It was Johnnie Mae who pulled the signal cord to bring us all to

Mrs. Mueller's beside. Johnnie was trembling. Sister Leota closed Mrs. Mueller's eyes, pulled the curtain around the bed, and guided Johnnie to a chair.

"Come on now," Florene said to me and we slipped inside the curtain. "Let's fix her up real nice." Our patient had slid against the bed rail when she died. Florene positioned one arm beneath Mrs. Mueller's shoulders and pulled her toward the center of the bed.

Below the bed rail's gray imprint on her forehead Mrs. Mueller's face was puffy. Her skin was white, but patches of blue grew on her ears and nose.

"Who will come to see her?" I asked.

"Her sister," Florene said. "Her husband is dead. No children that I know of."

"Husband . . . how long has he been dead?" And then the other questions I didn't ask: What time had we left her so carefully propped on pillows? Why hadn't I seen how oddly she lay pressed against the bed rail? Why were both eyes still open? We pulled Mrs. Mueller up in bed and the weight felt different, her arms limp and unresisting. I realized she had slumped against the bed rail at the moment when her body had given up.

"I don't know when her husband died," Florene said. "Look in the closet and see if there is a robe or scarf or something."

In her suitcase were three negligees: pink, white, and blue. I picked up the pink nylon; it smelled sweet, like roses.

"Look," I called to Florene.

"You never know," she smiled. "Too hard to put on though."

In one of the suitcase pockets I found two tortoiseshell hair combs. Brushing a dead woman's hair was not much different than brushing a live woman's hair. I tucked thin wisps of white hair up into the combs. Florene washed Mrs. Mueller's face, plucked a few hairs from her chin, and gave her a clean gown.

Before they went to lunch, Florene and Johnnie Mae combed their own hair and sprayed on some cologne. "Don't let me go like that," I heard Johnnie Mae say.

In the afternoon, we folded stacks of linen, mostly in silence. When Mrs. Mueller's sister arrived, I was wheeling a cart of fresh ice water from room to room. She wore a tailored gold suit with a matching veiled hat, but she was stooped and thin and walked

slowly down the hall with Sister Leota. I saw her bless herself be-
fore she went behind the curtain surrounding her sister's bed.

"Adele," I heard her say, and I thought about my sister, Car-
olyn, and the new pale green dress and heels she'd bought for her
graduation. "How do I look?" Carolyn had asked as she twirled
and tilted, so beautiful in the three-way mirror.

RX for Nurses: Brag!

KATHLEEN WALSH SPENCER *Bloomfield Hills, Michigan*

I am Alumnus of the Year from schools I've never heard of.
Colleges of Nursing send me diplomas. I have thirteen
honorary doctorates, two from Harvard Medical
in the same year!
Patients send so many letters of compliment, the hospital
expanded the mailroom, hired a secretary to open my mail.
Every administrator, employee, candystriper knows my name.
Patients ask for me: the nurse with the whitest shoes,
springiest step, the nurse who packs the best lunch
and brings homemade Jell-O in flavors the hospital chef
never dreamed of.
I am the nurse who can present a pureed lunch to a patient
and make him want to eat it!
I am the nurse who sneaks birthday cake out of the staff lounge
to share with patients! The pieces with the roses!
I am the nurse who serves up the tastiest soup that ever came
out of a can, with crackers I made at home
and carefully inserted into Nabisco packages.
I am champion of fluffing pillows, tightening sheets,
bending straws at the perfect angle.
And physical prowess is part of my charm.
I am the only one who has ever saved Resusci-Annie.
I can look through lead walls
to see a patient turn blue in the dark.
I can hear a call bell before the patient even pushes it.
I can hear a fly walk across an apple in a fruit basket
three doors down.
I'm Licensed, Registered, Certified, Certifiable.
I'm Nurse of the Year,
Nurse of the Decade.
If there were Nurse of the Millennium,
it would be me.

Sailor Explains Kissing the Nurse

KATHLEEN WALSH SPENCER *Bloomfield Hills, Michigan*

after V.J. Day at Times Square, *a photograph by Alfred Eisenstaedt*

I didn't care who she was, this cloud of white
against a sea of gray pavement littered with confetti
and crowds of sailors from Brooklyn Naval
in dress blues. Determined to kiss her,

I swept her into my arms like a wave foaming
over the bow of a patrol boat. I hooked my arm around her
shoulders and draped her so far backward,
one of her feet left dry land. How trusting

of her to dangle and return the kiss
of a stranger amidst the revelers. Office workers,
grandmothers, housewives, children — all stopped to smile
as I covered her mouth, nestled

her cheek against my shoulder as fiercely
as I'd protected a fresh pack of smokes from my grabby
bunk-mates. Her left arm slung back, her sleeve
a limp white flag of surrender.

Then Pop! Pop! a camera flash startled
us upright, she straightened her hem and needled
off through the crowd before the rewinding film
could even whir through the camera.

Army Nurses, Vietnam, 1966

KATHLEEN WALSH SPENCER *Bloomfield Hills, Michigan*

after the Vietnam Women's Memorial, *Washington, D.C., Glenna
Goodacre, Sculptor*

Too exhausted to swat the flies
that buzz their hair, three nurses
sit back to back on sandbags
to rest, to wait for the wounded
soldier to be choppered out, handed
over to the USS *Sanctuary* floating off Vietnam.

Among the bamboo trees of Phu Non, Vietnam,
one of the nurses holds the flyer,
stretches her arm, reaches her hand
across his chest: a pieta of nurse
and soldier, her limbs wound
around him to contain this awkward package

slipping from her grasp. She opens her bag,
wets her bandanna to shield him from Vietnam
sun, cools his forehead, covers his wounded
eyes until a surgeon can attempt repairs, mid-flight.
There is too much damage, but still she nurses,
grieving the loss of yet another handsome

face. To keep him on her lap, she grasps a handful
of the soldier's shirt. A plastic bag
rustles in his pocket. The nurse
peeks at the photo he carries in this jungle:
a young woman with flowing hair. *Fly High,
Love You,* she wrote with curlicues winding

into hearts. Placing the photo in its flimsy bag,
the nurse seals it, tucks it back, wounded.
The faces of all the Joes, Gerrys, Smittys, and Bobs fly

through her mind, blur with the rows of body bags
that carried them from Vietnam —
last words spoken, spoken to their nurse.

Lifting her chin, rising to full height, the second nurse
turns dark eyes to the sky. Hot wind
stirs the tight curls underneath her cap. In Vietnam,
unarmed, she reaches back to lay a hand
on her comrade's elbow, touching her baggy
sleeve, waiting for rescue, waiting to fly

out. The third nurse kneels, motionless as a butterfly
regaining strength after tearing from its silk cocoon.
The fine red dust of Vietnam coats her helmet, her hands.

Mercy

CONSTANCE STUDER *Boulder, Colorado*

Pick any day and stand by the ER door and you can see a frail man, unquestionably end-stage AIDS, or a woman holding a washcloth to her sliced finger. A prisoner from county jail with a bloody face, bruised chest, hands and ankles cuffed. Mothers, with their restless children in tow, looking ill at ease because they've lost their insurance. Streets around the hospital are always teeming. Nurses and techs have a smoke and a giggle in late August sun. Proud new mothers in oversized clothes bear small bundles to waiting cars. There is a small-town, campus feel to our hospital. Jazzed, vibrant, energizing, disturbing. Security guards and doctors and nurses struggle to control the comings and goings of patients who shout the mantra, *It hurts, oh, it hurts.*

My car throws a hub cap on the way to work, and there are police in the parking lot as I pull into my spot. "Here, I'll walk you in," the cop says, one hand on his gun. Up to the locker room. Loose-fitting white pants, white socks, white sneakers. Pink and blue t-shirt completes my ensemble. I close my locker door, clip my ID badge to my shirt. Past doors marked Radiology, Pathology, Nuclear Medicine. Then I swing through the doors of ICU, this never-never land where instruments vie for dominance over people. With a twirl of my swivel chair, I pour a cup of coffee and listen to the taped report, pen in hand, taking notes on my patients. Tanya Lewis was depressed and crying part of the night. I listen until the tape ends.

Working short-staffed again. Endless interruptions. Phone calls. Lab tests. IVs to be changed. Sterile dressings. Head-to-toe assessments. I'm passing nine o'clock meds and the moment that Tanya Lewis swallows, I realize that I just handed her the wrong pill. She is one of three patients I'm taking care of this Thursday. There had been six little white cups on the tray. My hand reached for the wrong one. Phones ring constantly. Computer screens glow with facts and figures. Doors open, close. Air hums with running feet, a high-tech symphony of beeps and buzzers.

The heat in the unit is amniotic. Tanya huddles in the corner of her bed, her anxious eyes darting from my hand holding her glass of water to the clock on the wall. "My husband is waiting outside. Will you let him in?" Rivulets of sweat roll down Tanya's forehead. Her heart rate is too rapid. A thin green tube forces oxygen into her nose. Her breath is short gasps. Wires under her gown tether her to the bedside monitor that chirps each erratic beat of her weakened heart.

I retreat to the med room, lean my head against the wall, close my eyes. All I want is to fold in on myself. The quiet dissolve. Fade to darkness. Float on an ocean of silence. All around, telephones ring. Dr. Bryant yells for a chart. Hands shaking, I walk to the waiting room where Tanya's husband has set up camp. He slept in the waiting room last night so he could see his wife for fifteen minutes every two hours.

"You may go in now, Bill," I say, holding the door open for him. He is tall, probably mid-forties, with brown hair thinning at the crown. His face is all angles and planes, a face a sculptor could do something with. His gray suit is wrinkled, his eyes tense with worry. He gathers up the briefcase that he uses as a pillow and hurries past me to his wife's bedside. He leans down to kiss her on the lips, and Tanya's face becomes radiant at the sight of him. Are you all right? they both say at the same moment, then both break out laughing. Bill sits on the edge of her bed all the while stroking her hair with his hand.

Maybe love is a gift given only to certain people, like perfect pitch or the ability to draw. And, as if in slow motion, over and over in my mind, I'm holding out Tanya's glass of water, watching as she draws up on the straw, swallows a pill not meant for her. No time for rules of passing medications: Right drug. Right time. Right dose. Right method of administration. Right patient. It's too late to take back my mistake. I've made my heart a desert and call it peace.

* * *

On my days off, I used to forget about all the wounds I'd seen at work by dancing at the Grizzly Rose. It was Friday night five years ago that I met him. The dance floor was hip-to-hip with men and women dressed in jeans and t-shirts and tank tops. Paulo had everyone's attention under the dazzle of strobe lights. He seduced me with his lithe body, narrow waist, small hips. Shoulder-length black hair swayed with each movement of his head. He danced like a sweaty angel, his body fluid against the harsh beat of the guitar. He spun, one hand waving free. All eyes were on him and he loved it.

"Come dance," he said, holding out his hand, pulling me onto the floor. He grabbed me around the waist and twirled me hard, pushed my body against his. He flirted, played with my hair, touched my waist and arms. Paulo was big with well-defined muscles, but he told me his history in the strength of his hands: *I was born in the mountains of Costa Rica. My family traveled six weeks to get to the states.*

Always, there was a sadness hovering behind his eyes. Sex was the one thing I'd gotten behind on the most and thought I could catch up on the quickest. Better than aspirin for what ailed me.

* * *

In ICU the lights are never turned off. In this windowless place, it's always "now." Sensory and stimuli-deprived patients lapse into confusion, ICU psychosis, floating in a haze of medication, pain, fear. The unit has six curtained cubicles, plus a glass-enclosed isolation room clustered around the nurses' station. Five rooms for coronary patients complete the other half of the circle. Each room has a monitor overhead for EKG readings, arterial lines, intracranial pressure readings. Suction equipment, blood pressure devices, rubbery IV bags with tubing snake through machines that count each drop. Nitro drip for pain control, antibiotic drip, straight in or piggybacked.

Alarms keep watch over everything. Something is always wrong. Ventilators beep when interrupted for suctioning and honk for pulmonary pressure changes. Patients long for the human touch of a bath, a walk, a conversation. No one thanks a nurse for flushing his central line. Monitors bong if a blood pressure is too high or too low. Even the beds are smart.

"Can I talk to you, Ann? Please?" Bill Lewis asks. I'm barreling through the unit with a load of clean linen in my right hand and a bottle of dextrose and water in my left. It's his hand on my arm that brings me to a halt.

"What can you tell me about Tanya's condition?" His smile is thin and tight.

"Her heart rate is still too fast. She's still running a significant fever, which is what has us worried."

Tanya has MS. As if that weren't enough, she also received a new mitral valve last month. Now, because of her increased risk of infections, we're watching her closely.

"Thank you. That's what I wanted to know. I'll be here if you need me," Bill says as he half bows out of the room. Through the glass door I watch him carefully remove his suit jacket, fold it in two, and place it on the chair next to the only sofa, settling in for a long wait.

I hurry on. Pass meds. Hang IVs. Transcribe orders. Constantly, we play the game of musical beds: Who is the sickest? Who can we move to make room for the gunshot wound in ER? Who can I bump over to the wards? So many times I've seen the signs of imminent death: A blurring of the body's boundaries, a gentle and sometimes not-so-gentle fusion with surrounding elements, a sigh into oblivion.

* * *

Someone has died on our unit every shift for a week. Monday it was Mrs. Tomlin, a woman with DIC, a bleeding disorder, Lucy's patient, who, it turns out, received the wrong blood. She bled out and died and no one wanted to do CPR, no one wanted their name on her chart because her husband swore he'd sue. Blood is a smell the brain never forgets, a smell that goes straight to some deep primitive center of the cortex. We had a meeting to discuss the circumstances around her death: *Did I do the right thing? Could I have done something different to change the situation?*

A thirty-year-old waitress shot herself and died four days later, her face caved in. Tiny glinting pieces of human tissue mixed with crimson splatters. Lance, an eighteen-year-old, was admitted for a hernia repair and went into cardiac arrest on the OR table. He is one of my patients today, too. Brain-stem dysfunction. No pupillary light reflex, no gag reflex, no spontaneous respirations. Doll's eyes response, the neurologist wrote on his chart. As I bathe Lance, the room is filled with the rhythmic sound of the respirator, its small protective glass cage misted with condensation, its black balloon collapsing and refilling, inhaling and exhaling, making its fist and opening to its blossom, over and over again. Lucy and Carol fly by on their way to their own private emergencies, their faces full of determination. Nothing we do is ever enough.

* * *

Paulo was eight years younger. We had an immediate understanding. I never had to explain my life to him. He got what I was about. Paulo, splendid in his white linen suit, dark limpid eyes. Romantic without being controlling. After all my one-night stands, I believed romance was a patriarchal plot to hide women behind thick walls and to hook us into bearing lots of male children. I'd fallen in love about once a month before I met Paulo. Sex, that weaving dance of give and take, the swirling of minds, the dip and sway of dreams, dance of the senses. All of a sudden I wasn't looking over his left shoulder wondering about the next encounter with someone else.

Paulo won me over with his hands. We were in the shower, soaping each other's backs. Peppermint soap, the smell, the tingling. We slid around on each other's skin and morning sun shone into the shower through the hanging plants. Water sparkled on our naked bodies as we splashed. And all at once we were in a jungle waterfall cavorting among vines and rocks. Wild animals. We began to growl and paw each other's bodies. I grabbed Paulo and started to lick him all over, from the bottom of his backbone and moving up his spine. Tiger woman, he called me. Tiger man, I growled back. We stepped out of the shower and shook water out of our hair, rolled our bodies dry on big shaggy towels. We moved from bedroom to living room to kitchen.

The bed was our cave. No boundaries. Not an inch, inside or out, that we didn't explore. What is love but imagination that gives, takes, breathes and has room, like skin, to expand?

* * *

Tanya lies in bed talking to her husband and looks OK. Is it a mistake only if I get caught? The unit is quiet, almost becalmed. I sit with Lucy and Carol in the nurses' station, our island comprising two long desks equipped with computers and phones and monitors. Dr. Logan, Tanya's doctor, walks in. He is the one I must tell.

"Do you have a minute?"

"Only one," he says, following me into the conference room. I shut the door.

"I gave Tanya Lewis Lanoxin instead of Lasix this morning. I'll make out an incident report." Lanoxin is a form of digitalis given to slow and strengthen the heartbeat. Lasix helps remove excess fluid.

"Is this the first time you've ever given someone the wrong medicine?" Dr. Logan asks in his I'm-the-doctor-you're-the-peon tone of voice. His skin is the color of ash.

"As far as I know. I knew the moment I saw her swallow the pill. I feel terrible."

"Don't tell anyone. No sense asking for a lawsuit," he says. I look at him in amazement, then remember to whom I'm speaking. This is the doctor who wrote an order for 50 mgm of Demerol to be given intravenously to Sylvia, one of our patients admitted in respiratory distress. She was coughing up bright blood from her ravaged lungs. Ventilator. Twenty-one years old. Ill for two weeks with "flu." I had known he must have meant IM instead of IV. Fifty milligrams of Demerol intravenously would kill her. I called him and asked him to change the order. He flew into a rage.

"How could you question my order?" he yelled.

I called Barbara, our head nurse, who called Dr. Logan and explained the situation in her most diplomatic style. He told her to go to hell. He threatened to have her fired. Give the drug as ordered, he insisted. As a last resort, Barbara called the chief of medicine at home. He put a hold on Dr. Logan's order instead of canceling it, but refused to prescribe another analgesic to take its place. So Sylvia went without pain medication for over twenty-four hours because her doctor wouldn't admit he'd made a mistake.

"Doctor, you haven't heard a word I've said," I say as I rise to leave. When does memory stop being blame?

* * *

I keep finding excuses to check on Tanya. She's laughing with her husband. "So how are you feeling?" I ask as I adjust the drops-per-minute on her IVAC. Her heart rate on the monitor is slower, more regular. "I'm better now that Bill is here," Tanya says. She's breathing more easily. Her skin is dry. Maybe her fever has finally broken. Bill runs a brush through her long brown hair.

"Isn't she beautiful?" Bill says.

"Quit," Tanya says, but her eyes say, *Tell me more.*

"This isn't a beauty contest," I say.

"Good thing," Tanya laughs. I exit around the curtain as Tanya lays her head on Bill's chest and he rubs her back. Standing there watching them, I'm jealous of how in love they are. Wanting to be wanted. Listened to. Really listened to, the way Paulo listened to me. I could say anything—*I bought peas for dinner*, or *My car needs an oil change*. It was the way he looked at me when I talked. Suddenly, I wasn't talking about my car anymore. I was revealing everything I ever knew about myself. The girls I used to jump rope with, the tree I laid under as a child, my first kiss. The way I pushed my hair back from my forehead, knitted my brow, tightened my lips when I was trying to remember a name. Love was a sudden look of appreciation. He noticed everything, so I dressed for him, bathed for him, put on perfume and makeup. I felt known. No longer just one woman in the multitude, I was unique. Me. That was what it felt like to be loved.

When I go to the utility room to empty a urine bag, I feel dizzy and think I'm going to pass out. No lunch. All I can see is Tanya with her eyes rolling back into her head and her monitor straightlining and me pushing the "COR O" button and putting the head of Tanya's bed down, giving her quick breaths, starting chest compressions. "COR O, ICU" the paging system shouts. Feet run. The team crowds around her bed. Her gown slips down revealing her chest. Commotion escalates. She's in V-fib. Death, the great equalizer, the great surprise.

"Are you all right?" Lucy asks, as she watches me peeking through Tanya's door. Tanya is mulling over her choices on the menu. Bill is changing the music on her CD player, helping her put the earphones back on.

"No. I'm not," I say.

"Anything I can do?" Lucy asks as she pushes her curly brunette hair behind her ears.

"It's something I've got to work out for myself." Other scenes pass before my eyes: Standing in front of the director of nursing as she tells me I'm fired. Being hauled before the State Nursing Board —*Your nursing license has been revoked.* Slinging hash at Salinger's Diner.

* * *

Colorado air is always in motion, sometimes a chinook blast, sometimes a gentle January whisper. A hushabye soughing of piñon pines nearby. Paulo had a little cabin by Grand Lake. It was about ten degrees when I got there. Snow squeaked under my heels. The hairs in my nostrils vibrated like wind chimes. The cabin was one room with an old black and silver potbellied stove in the center. When I opened the door, heat drew me in. He had candles on the table and soup simmering on the stove. The smell of beef and carrots and onions, such comfort. After all those years of tension and taking care of everyone else in the universe, I couldn't say a word.

Paulo reached for my hand and led me to the mattress on the floor. "Let me give you a massage," he said. I accepted, and he gently stripped me to the skin before I could think. I was lying on Paulo's bed, naked, with my arms plastered to my sides. My stomach was tense. I laid there with my eyes shut, and heard him stoke the stove and put a bottle of massage oil to warm in a pan of water. Then he moved behind me on the mattress, slid his back against the wall and straddled my body. He placed his big incredibly warm hands under my neck. He held them there and leaned over and whispered into my ear, "Remember to breathe."

His breath was like sweet grass. "Listen for my breathing and then breathe along with me." I forced myself to take in air and expel it, so at least I'd look as if I were alive. Then he sat up and poured warm oil into his palms. The room filled with a healing smell I remembered from childhood. The kind that clears out your sinuses in a whiff.

He slid his hands down my shoulders and arms and, in the same motion, pulled me up from the waist, lifted my body and spread my ribcage so that I finally did begin to breathe, gulping in air down to my toes. I opened my eyes and looked up at him, into that strong-boned, upside-down face. The whites of his eyes were so clear they were almost blue.

"What are you doing?" I whispered.

"I'm showing you how love feels," he said.

There seemed to be less and less space between us, as if we were becoming one rhythm. His hands found my stomach. He drizzled warm oil onto my belly, drew a line up my body, ever so slowly, up to my throat and chin and nose and forehead. Solemn, deliberate, like an initiation ceremony. He slid his body on top of mine, bellies touching, warm breath in each other's ears. A cry came from my mouth that would have awakened wolves or coyotes, if there had been any left in the woods.

* * *

"Go grab some lunch," Lucy says. "I'll cover your patients. I'm worried about you." Our last admission, a transfer from a surgical floor, has settled in. The nurses' station is empty of doctors. The orders on the charts have been transcribed and hung back in their slots.

"Keep an eye on Tanya Lewis, okay?" I say. Lucy shoos me off with a wave of her hand as she flies through the nurses' station on her way to answer a light.

Down the elevator. The cafeteria is a cave carved out in the basement. The smell is of too many burned pans of macaroni and cheese. I grab a tray and force my mind to decide between rigid spaghetti and limp salad. I settle for chicken noodle soup.

"Come sit with me," Bill says. He has a full tray of spaghetti drowned in parmesan cheese, garlic bread.

"How can you look so good after being here so many hours, Bill?"

"As long as I'm near Tanya, I'm okay," he says as he makes room for me at his table. I fall into the seat. Only now do I feel how tired my muscles are.

"Have you and Tanya been married long?"

"Five years. I met her at a pottery show. She was selling some of her work. All I saw was her gorgeous smile and blue eyes. Then her wheelchair. It was her incredible spirit that I fell in love with. But it's still hard sometimes," Bill says, setting down his fork, his eyes clouded by worry. "Her MS is our illness. When do you think she'll be able to move out of ICU?"

"Soon. I think." I pick my words carefully. The hot soup scalds my tongue.

"COR O, ICU. COR O, ICU" the PA system blares. Bill and I look at each other then run for the stairs. Please Lord don't let it be Tanya, I pray. When I race into the unit, the new admit from the surgical floor is in full cardiac arrest. Lucy is on the top of the bed doing chest compressions. Carol is ambuing. The ER doctor is talking with the attending. They call the code: time of death, 2:46 P.M. I'm ashamed how relieved I am that it's not Tanya. Grief is a train that doesn't run on anyone else's schedule. Medicine turns grief into a set of rules, stages, deadlines, tucking messy emotions under neat clinical labels: Trauma. Pain. Detachment. Acceptance. Time's up.

The wife and daughter come and Lucy leads them behind the beige curtain where their loved one lies. They emerge a half hour later wiping their eyes, bearing his belongings in a plastic bag. Mother and daughter lean against each other, like the twin braces of a house. One wrong move by either of them and their support will cave in. Watching them, my heart aches and my throat almost shuts. Over and over I've witnessed grief, the breath checked and the heart belabored, the eyes giving up their tears, the tongue as bitter as if it had tasted poison.

Voices float in from the corridor. Someone laughs. Trays litter bedside tables. IVACs pump like heartbeats. All around me swirl life and death issues. Mrs. Lanowski — long history of diabetes, admitted with gas gangrene of her right leg — has lapsed into total body failure: lungs, liver, kidney.

I turn her onto her right side, put a pillow behind her back, between her legs, carefully, as if the fragile bones might snap. Her feet are purple and cold to the touch. In the cubicle next to her is Larry Thompson, an eighteen-year-old boy whose brain is gone because he refused to wear a motorcycle helmet. They lie side-by-side, facing opposite directions, like angry lovers.

* * *

In the past six months, three nurses from our unit have resigned. Last weekend, Barbara threw a party for Marie. Joni Mitchell was singing: At last, my love has come along. Margaritas flowed like tap water; the table was heavy with homemade bread and pecan pie and fried chicken and ambrosia salad. I lounged on the floor next to the guest of honor.

"Did you hear the latest? They want to do mastectomies on an outpatient basis, amputate and out," Carol said as she licked chicken from her fingers.

"Lord help us. A woman goes into surgery anxious about life and death and mutilation. She comes out with a wound, pain, tubes, and psychological trauma. And they want to do drive-through mastectomies," Lucy said.

"So aren't you going to miss all this fun when you're selling real estate, Marie?" Carol asked.

"No. The last month of nights almost did me in."

"Give her a year and she'll be back," Lucy said. "She'll miss all the great food at our parties."

"Don't count on it. Too few nurses. Not enough money. Sicker patients. Who cares anyway? Where are the raised voices coming over radio waves and TV screens and newsstand headlines? If no one else cares, why should we?" Marie said. She sprang to her feet and waved her empty margarita glass in the air like a flag of surrender.

* * *

An August wedding by Grand Lake. Paulo in white cotton pants and flowing shirt. Me in a long white cotton skirt and peasant blouse which I wore off my shoulders. Baby white roses woven into my long brown braids. Friends formed a circle around us as we said our vows: I promise to realize my full potential for both closeness and autonomy, to hold nothing back, to tell the truth, to listen nonjudgmentally to what you say. I am responsible for my own happiness, well-being, life-goals. I love you as you are this moment. Then we danced and sang along with a live band. For Paulo, romance was much more than a bouquet of roses. The day we married, Paulo brought me a Tibetan singing bowl that glowed with the softness and sheen of silk.

"This bowl was crafted in the high mountains from seven holy metals," he explained. "I see this bowl as a symbol for you, the woman I love. You are strong, like this bowl, round, with no corners or projectiles. Powerful like an open hand, not a closed fist. Listen," he said as he began to stroke the rim with a wooden dowel. The bowl was simple with no decoration, but had a voice that opened the heart. We breathed together and listened until the sound reached our bones. It was a barely audible contralto, yet vibrant enough to waffle the eardrums, wring tears from my eyes. A voice of heartbeat, the hum the earth sings.

There is a constant shuffle of patients. Every time an alarm goes off, Carol or Lucy or I race to see whose patient is in trouble. Eyeballing monitors as I race through the nurses' station with a load of linen or an IV to be hung is second nature. At its best, ICU is the finest medicine has to offer, swift intervention to save a life. At its worst, it is not so much life preserved as death prolonged. I feel a fluttery touch on my back. It's the daughter of a woman who was transferred in from 4 North with a high fever. Probably sepsis.

"Please. Get my mother something for pain," her daughter pleads. I leaf through her chart and read the pathology report: Liver cancer. Dorothy Simms is all bone and eyes and yellow skin. I search the med sheet for the time and amount of her last dose of pain medicine. I scan the nurses' notes and read *patient requesting pain med. Dr. Solano called for order. Order refused.*

"Why hasn't your mother been receiving pain meds?" I ask.

"I don't know what to do," the daughter says as she stands twisting the edge of her sweater between white fingers.

"The physician is working with you and your mother, and you have the right to be part of the decision-making team," I say, reaching for the phone. I call and am put on hold, wait, then listen as Dr. Solano tells me that Dorothy has been trying to get narcotics from day one.

"I'll be in to see her," he says as the phone clicks.

"But she has cancer," I say to the dead phone.

"Sorry. Dr. Solano is coming in. I can't do anything until he gets here." The daughter lowers her eyes, all guilty humility. She retreats to sit beside her mother's bed. There is no Book of Right Answers. All I can think about is whether or not I should tell Tanya Lewis about my mistake. I'm afraid.

* * *

Just last week, before Paulo went to visit his brother in Costa Rica, I helped him strip the apple trees before the season's first snow would shock the fruits into mush. The glossiest apples graced a white bowl. For Paulo, cooking was instinctual, his movements quick and sure. About this much flour, he'd say, tapping the bowl. And a handful of sugar. It was the warmth of his hands that did it in the end, pressing and kneading. Cooking, like nursing, is all about hands, ladling out, putting in, touching. Hands will always be needed. Paulo's dumplings glimmer in the depths of my freezer, waiting to be discovered on a bitter-cold winter night, pale doughy globes with summer in their hearts.

* * *

"Are you ready for your bath?" I ask. Tanya lies peacefully reading a book. She looks better than she has for days. Her skin glows. Maybe the Lanoxin did her some good, or maybe that's just wishful thinking. Maybe it was seeing her husband. There is a hand-thrown pottery bowl on her bedside table.

"I'm ready if you are," Tanya says with a smile. I fill the basin with warm soapy water, gather her towel and washcloth, lower the head of her bed. "My husband told me to tell you that he appreciates how you keep him informed about my condition. He has a hard time reaching Dr. Logan."

"Did Bill bring the bowl?" I ask as I wash Tanya's right arm, up and back, then dry it with a towel. Tanya reads the expression on my face.

"I know, I know, I can't keep it in ICU, but yes, it's one of mine. Bill wants me home, fast, and he knows the best way is to remind me of my passion. There's nothing like the feel of clay as I form it by hand on the potter's wheel. Days fly by when I'm wedging clay, rolling, paddling, coiling it to get out the air. When I get into the rhythm, it's like meditation."

"Is it hard to learn?" I drape her legs with the bath blanket. Her right leg is withered, muscles atrophied. But her arm muscles are hard and well-defined by years of rolling along in her wheelchair. "The trickiest part is putting the pot into the first fire, the bisque, embedding it in sawdust, firing it, letting it go to the elements, wind, rain, snow, whatever comes along. I never know what I'm going to end up with. It's when the pots crack in two in the kiln that I learn the most."

"It's a beautiful bowl. My husband loved pottery. He gave me a singing bowl once." Done with her legs, I start to wash her back. Through the curtain I can hear Lucy's voice as she tapes her report for the evening nurses, her voice slow and tired, a kind of choral sigh.

I pull up a chair beside Tanya's bed, open my mouth to tell her about my mistake, and when I hear Dr. Solano in the nurses' station yelling at Carol, I think of Paulo lost in Costa Rica no one knows where. About the flood that wiped out the village where his brother lived. My silence is the grief of not knowing whether Paulo is still alive, of trying to forgive myself for all my mistakes, a prayer for mercy. At night when I can't sleep, I run my finger around the rim of the singing bowl and hear Paulo's voice saying *relax breathe feel let go of control. Be open to the outcome. My spirit is here in this room.* No healing comes without cost. Harm happens. No one is immune.

We Do Abortions Here: A Nurse's Story

SALLIE TISDALE *Portland, Oregon*

We do abortions here; that is all we do. There are weary, grim moments when I think I cannot bear another basin of bloody remains, utter another kind phrase of reassurance. So I leave the procedure room in the back and reach for a new chart. Soon I am talking to an eighteen-year-old woman pregnant for the fourth time. I push up her sleeve to check her blood pressure and find row upon row of needle marks, neat and parallel and discolored. She has been so hungry for her drug for so long that she has taken to using the loose skin of her upper arms; her elbows are already a permanent ruin of bruises. She is surprised to find herself nearly four months pregnant. I suspect she is often surprised, in a mild way, by the blows she is dealt. I prepare myself for another basin, another brief and chafing loss.

"How can you stand it?" Even the clients ask. They see the machine, the strange instruments, the blood, the final stroke that wipes away the promise of pregnancy. Sometimes I see that too: I watch a woman's swollen abdomen sink to softness in a few stuttering moments and my own belly flip-flops with sorrow. But all it takes for me to catch my breath is another interview, one more story that sounds so much like the last one. There is a numbing sameness lurking in this job: the same questions, the same answers, even the same trembling tone in the voices. The worst is the sameness of human failure, of inadequacy in the face of each day's dull demands.

In describing this work, I find it difficult to explain how much I enjoy it most of the time. We laugh a lot here, as friends and as professional peers. It's nice to be with women all day. I like the sudden, transient bonds I forge with some clients: moments when I am in my strength, remembering weakness, and a woman in weakness reaches out for my strength. What I offer is not power, but solidness, offered almost eagerly. Certain clients waken in me every tender urge I have — others make me wince and bite my tongue. Both challenge me to find a balance. It is a sweet brutality we practice here, a stark and loving dispassion.

I look at abortion as if I am standing on a cliff with a telescope, gazing at some great vista. I can sweep the horizon with both eyes, survey the scene in all its distance and size. Or I can put my eye to the lens and focus on the small details, suddenly so close. In abortion the absolute must always be tempered by the contextual, because both are real, both valid, both hard. How can we do this? How can we refuse? Each abortion is a measure of our failure to protect, to nourish our own. Each basin I empty is a promise — but a promise broken a long time ago.

I grew up on the great promise of birth control. Like many women my age, I took the pill as soon as I was sexually active. To risk pregnancy when it was so easy to avoid seemed stupid, and my contraceptive success, as it were, was part of the promise of social enlightenment. But birth control fails, far more frequently than laboratory trials predict. Many of our clients take the pill; its failure to protect them is a shocking realization. We have clients who have been sterilized, whose husbands have had vasectomies; each one is a statistical misfit, fine print come to life. The anger and shame of these women I hold in one hand, and the basin in the other. The distance between the two, the length I pace and try to measure, is the size of an abortion.

The procedure is disarmingly simple. Women are surprised, as though the mystery of conception, a dark and hidden genesis, requires an elaborate finale. In the first trimester of pregnancy, it's a mere few minutes of vacuuming, a neat tidying up. I give a woman a small yellow Valium, and when it has begun to relax her, I lead her into the back, into bareness, the stirrups. The doctor reaches in her, opening the narrow tunnel to the uterus with a succession of slim, smooth bars of steel. He inserts a plastic tube and hooks it to a hose on the machine. The woman is framed against white paper that crackles as she moves, the light bright in her eyes. Then the machine rumbles low and loud in the small windowless room; the doctor moves the tube back and forth with an efficient rhythm, and the long tail of it fills with blood that spurts and stumbles along into a jar. He is usually finished in a few minutes. They are long minutes for the woman; her uterus frequently reacts to its abrupt emptying with a powerful, unceasing cramp which cuts off the blood vessels and enfolds the irritated, bleeding tissue.

I am learning to recognize the shadows that cross the faces of the women I hold. While the doctor works between her spread legs, the paper drape hiding his intent expression, I stand beside the table. I hold the woman's hands in mine, resting them just below her ribs. I watch her eyes, finger her necklace, stroke her hair. I ask about her job, her family; in a haze she answers me; we chatter, faces close, eyes meeting and sliding apart.

I watch the shadows that creep up unnoticed and suddenly darken her face as she screws up her features and pushes a tear out each side to slide down her cheeks. I have learned to anticipate the quiver of chin, the rapid intake of breath, and the surprising sobs that rise soon after the machine starts to drum. I know this is when the cramp deepens, and the tears are partly the tears that follow pain — the sharp, childish crying when one bumps one's head on a cabinet door. But a well of woe seems to open beneath many women when they hear that thumping sound. The anticipation of the moment has finally come to fruit; the moment has arrived when the loss is no longer an imagined one. It has come true.

I am struck by the sameness and I am struck every day by the variety here — how this commonplace dilemma can so display the differences of women. A twenty-one-year-old woman, unemployed, uneducated, without family, in the fifth month of her fifth pregnancy. A forty-two-year-old mother of teenagers, shocked by her condition, refusing to tell her husband. A twenty-three-year-old mother of two having her seventh abortion, and many women in their thirties having their first. Some are stoic, some hysterical, a few giggle uncontrollably, many cry.

I talk to a sixteen-year-old uneducated girl who was raped. She has gonorrhea. She describes blinding headaches, attacks of breathlessness, nausea. "Sometimes I feel like two different people," she tells me with a calm smile, "and I talk to myself."

I pull out my plastic models. She listens patiently for a time, and then holds her hands wide in front of her stomach.

"When's the baby going to go up into my stomach?" she asks.

I blink. "What do you mean?"

"Well," she says, still smiling, "when women get so big, isn't the baby in your stomach? Doesn't it hatch out of an egg there?"

My first question in an interview is always the same. As I walk down the hall with the woman, as we get settled in chairs and I glance through her files, I am trying to gauge her, to get a sense of the words, and the tone, I should use. With some I joke, with others I chat, sometimes I fall into a brisk, business-like patter. But I ask every woman, "Are you sure you want to have an abortion?" Most nod with grim knowing smiles. "Oh, yes," they sigh. Some seek forgiveness, offer excuses. Occasionally a woman will flinch and say, "Please don't use that word."

Later I describe the procedure to come, using care with my language. I don't say "pain" any more than I would say "baby." So many are afraid to ask how much it will hurt. "My sister told me — " I hear. "A friend of mine said — " and the dire expectations unravel. I prick the index finger of a woman for a drop of blood to test, and as the tiny lancet approaches the skin she averts her eyes, holding her trembling hand out to me and jumping at my touch.

It is when I am holding a plastic uterus in one hand, a suction tube in the other, moving them together in imitation of the scrubbing to come, that women ask the most secret questions. I am speaking in a matter-of-fact voice about "the tissue" and "the contents" when the woman suddenly catches my eye and asks, "How big is the baby now?" These words suggest a quiet need for a definition of the boundaries being drawn. It isn't so odd, after all, that she feels relief when I describe the growing bud's bulbous shape, its miniature nature. Again I gauge, and sometimes lie a little, weaseling around its infantile features until its clinging power slackens.

But when I look in the basin, among the curdlike blood clots, I see an elfin thorax, attenuated, its pencilline ribs all in parallel rows with tiny knobs of spine rounding upwards. A translucent arm and hand swim beside.

A sleepy-eyed girl, just fourteen, watched me with a slight and goofy smile all through her abortion. "Does it have little feet and little fingers and all?" she'd asked earlier. When the suction was over she sat up woozily at the end of the table and murmured, "Can I see it?" I shook my head firmly.

"It's not allowed," I told her sternly, because I knew she didn't really want to see what was left. She accepted this statement of authority, and a shadow of confused relief crossed her plain, pale face.

Privately, even grudgingly, my colleagues might admit the power of abortion to provoke emotion. But they seem to prefer the broad view and disdain the telescope. Abortion is a matter of choice, privacy, control. Its uncertainty lies in specific cases: retarded women and girls too young to give consent for surgery, women who are ill or hostile or psychopathic. Such common dilemmas are met with both compassion and impatience: they slow things down. We are too busy to chew over ethics. One person might discuss certain concerns, behind closed doors, or describe a particularly disturbing dream. But generally there is no ambivalence.

Every day I take calls from women who are annoyed that we cannot see them, cannot do their abortion today, this morning, now. They argue the price, demand that we stay after hours to accommodate their job or class schedule. Abortion is so routine that one expects it to be like a manicure: quick, cheap, and painless.

Still, I've cultivated a certain disregard. It isn't negligence, but I don't always pay attention. I couldn't be here if I tried to judge each case on its merits; after all, we do over a hundred abortions a week. At some point each individual in this line of work draws a boundary and adheres to it. For one physician the boundary is a particular week of gestation; for another, it is a certain number of repeated abortions. But these boundaries can be fluid too: one physician overruled his own limit to abort a mature but severely malformed fetus. For me, the limit is allowing my clients to carry their own burden, shoulder the responsibility themselves. I shoulder the burden of trying not to judge them.

This city has several "crisis pregnancy centers" advertised in the yellow pages. They are small offices staffed by volunteers, and they offer free pregnancy testing, glossy photos of dead fetuses, and movies. I had a client recently whose mother is active in the anti-abortion movement. The young woman went to the local crisis center and was told that the doctor would make her touch her dismembered baby, that the pain would be the most horrible she could imagine, and that she might, after an abortion, never be able to have children. All lies. They called her at home and at work, over and over and over, but she had been wise enough to give a false name. She came to us a fugitive. We who do abortions are marked, by some, as impure. It's dirty work.

When a deliveryman comes to the sliding glass window by the reception desk and tilts a box toward me, I hesitate. I read the packing slip, assess the shape and weight of the box in light of its supposed contents. We request familiar faces. The doors are carefully locked; I have learned to half glance around at bags and boxes, looking for a telltale sign. I register with security when I arrive, and I am careful not to bang a door. We are all a little on edge here.

Concern about size and shape seem to be natural, and so is the relief that follows. We make the powerful assumption that the fetus is different from us, and even when we admit the similarities, it is too simplistic to be seduced by form alone. But the form is enormously potent—humanoid, powerless, palm-sized, and pure, it evokes an almost fierce tenderness when viewed simply as what it appears to be. But appearance, and even potential, aren't enough. The fetus, in becoming itself, can ruin others; its utter dependence has a sinister side. When I am struck in the moment by the contents in the basin, I am careful to remember the context, to note the tearful teenager and the woman sighing with something more than relief. One kind of question, though, I find considerably trickier.

"Can you tell what it is?" I am asked, and this means gender. This question is asked by couples, not women alone. Always couples would abort a girl and keep a boy. I have been asked about twins, and even if I could tell what race the father was.

An eighteen-year-old woman with three daughters brought her husband to the interview. He glared first at me, then at his wife, as he sank lower and lower in the chair, picking his teeth with a toothpick. He interrupted a conversation with his wife to ask if I could tell whether the baby would be a boy or a girl. I told him I could not.

"Good," he replied in a slow and strangely malevolent voice, "'cause if it was a boy I'd wring her neck."

In a literal sense, abortion exists because we are able to ask such questions, able to assign a value to the fetus which can shift with changing circumstances. If the human bond to a child were as primitive and unflinchingly narrow as that of other animals, there would be no abortion. There would be no abortion because then there would be nothing more important than caring for the young and perpetuating the species, no reason for sex but to make babies. I sense this sometimes, this wordless organic duty, when I do ultrasounds.

We do an ultrasound, a sound-wave test that paints a gray picture of the fetus, whenever we're uncertain of gestation. Age is measured by the width of the skull and confirmed by the length of the femur or thighbone; we speak of a pregnancy as being a certain "femur length" in weeks. The usual concern is whether a pregnancy is within the legal limit for an abortion. Women this far along have bellies which swell out round and tight like trim muscles. When they lie flat, the mound rises softly above the hips, pressing the umbilicus upward.

It takes practice to read an ultrasound picture, which is grainy and etched as though in strokes of charcoal. But suddenly a rapid rhythmic motion appears — the beating heart. Nearby is a soft oval, scratched with lines — the skull. The leg is harder to find, and then suddenly the fetus moves, bobbing in the surf. The skull turns away, an arm slides across the screen, the torso rolls. I know the weight of a baby's head on my shoulder, the whisper of lips on ears, the delicate curve of a fragile spine in my hand. I know how heavy and correct a cradled newborn feels. The creature I watch in secret requires nothing from me but to be left alone, and that is precisely what won't be done.

These inadvertently made beings are caught in a twisting web of motive and desire. They are at least inconvenient, sometimes quite literally dangerous in the womb, but most often they fall somewhere in between — consequences never quite believed in come to roost. Their virtue rises and falls outside their own nature: they become only what we make them. A fetus created by accident is the most absolute kind of surprise. Whether the blame lies in a failed IUD, a slipped condom, or a false impression of safety, that fetus is a thing whose creation has been actively worked against. Its existence is now an error. I think this is why so few women, even late in a pregnancy, will consider giving a baby up for adoption. To do so means making the fetus real — imagining it as something whole and outside oneself. The decision to terminate a pregnancy is sometimes so difficult and confounding that it creates an enormous demand for immediate action. The decision is a rejection; the pregnancy has become something to be rid of, a condition to be ended. It is a burden, a weight, a thing separate.

Women have abortions because they are too old, and too

young, too poor, and too rich, too stupid, and too smart. I see women who berate themselves with violent emotions for their first and only abortion, and others who return three times, five times, hauling two or three children, who cannot remember to take a pill or where they put the diaphragm. We talk glibly about choice. But the choice for what? I see all the broken promises in lives lived like a series of impromptu obstacles. There are sweet, light promises of love and intimacy, the glittering promise of education and progress, the warm promise of safe families, long years of innocence and community. And there is the promise of freedom: freedom from failure, from faithlessness. Freedom from biology. The early feminist defense of abortion asked many questions, but the one I remember is this: is biology destiny? And the answer is yes, sometimes it is. Women who have the fewest choices of all exercise their right to abortion the most.

Oh, the ignorance. I take a woman to the back room and ask her to undress; a few minutes later I return and find her positioned discreetly behind a drape, still wearing underpants. "Do I have to take these off too?" she asks, a little shocked. Some swear they have not had sex; many do not know what a uterus is, how sperm and egg meet, how sex makes babies. Some late seekers do not believe themselves pregnant; they believe themselves *impregnable*. I was chastised when I began this job for referring to some clients as girls: it is a feminist heresy. They come so young, snapping gum, sockless and sneakered, and their shakily applied eyeliner smudges when they cry. I call them girls with maternal benignity. I cannot imagine them as mothers.

The doctor seats himself between the woman's thighs and reaches into the dilated opening of a five-month pregnant uterus. Quickly he grabs and crushes the fetus in several places, and the room is filled with a low clatter and snap of forceps, the click of the tenaculum, and a pulling, sucking sound. The paper crinkles as the drugged and sleepy woman shifts, the nurse's low, honey-brown voice explains each step in delicate words.

I have fetus dreams. We all do here: dreams of abortions one after the other; of buckets of blood splashed on the walls; trees full of crawling fetuses. I dreamed that two men grabbed me and began to drag me away. "Let's do an abortion," they said with a sickening leer, and I began to scream, plunged into a vision of sucking, scraping pain, of being spread and torn by impartial instruments that do only what they are bidden. I woke from this dream barely able to breathe and thought of kitchen tables and coat hangers, knitting needles striped with blood, and women all alone clutching a pillow in their teeth to keep the screams from piercing the apartment-house walls. Abortion is the narrowest edge between kindness and cruelty. Done as well as it can be, it is still violence — merciful violence, like putting a suffering animal to death.

Maggie, one of the nurses, received a call at midnight not long ago. It was a woman in the twentieth week of pregnancy; the necessarily gradual process of cervical dilation begun the day before had stimulated labor, as it sometimes does. Maggie and one of the doctors met the woman at the office in the night. Maggie helped her onto the table, and as she lay down the fetus was delivered into Maggie's hands. When Maggie told me about it the next day, she cupped her hands into a small bowl — "It was just like a little kitten," she said softly, wonderingly. "Everything was still attached."

At the end of the day I clean out the suction jars, pouring blood into the sink, splashing the sides with flecks of tissue. From the sink rises a rich and humid smell, hot, earthy, and moldering: it is the smell of something recently alive beginning to decay. I take care of the plastic tub on the floor, filled with pieces too big to be trusted to the trash. The law defines the contents of the bucket I hold protectively against my chest as "tissue." Some would say my complicity in filling that bucket gives me no right to call it anything else. I slip the tissue gently into a bag and place it in the freezer, to be burned at another time. Abortion requires of me an entirely new set of assumptions. It requires a willingness to live with conflict, fearlessness, and grief. As I close the freezer door, I imagine a world where this won't be necessary, and then return to the world where it is.

The Door Locker

JANET TRIPP *Minneapolis, Minnesota*

It's a Monday after a holiday weekend. Our psychiatric unit is filled beyond capacity. Twenty-two patients when we should only have twenty-one.

Sylvia, slicing away at herself. First her forearm, then her stomach. She'd never cut her stomach before.

DeDe, dismissive and loud, but at least she talks to me now. Even though I helped strap her down. Even though I helped give her the shot. Even though I'm the enemy, she will look me in the eye and ask for cigarettes, a tube of toothpaste, the time of day.

Hank, lying in bed until two of us insist that he get up. I lock his door so he can't sneak back to bed before I air it out and the urine has dried.

Asmait, stabilized on her meds now, but still not well enough to go home, which is what she wants. Her seven children wait for her. She paces the floor and cries on the phone as she talks to them.

Natisha says she is fine so I will leave her alone. Then she goes into her room and screams and snarls at the voices. When I knock, she replies in her sweetest voice, "I'm fine. I'm fine."

Rufus knows he must take his meds or the security guards — the enforcers — will be called to stand behind us until the medicine is in him by one means or another. But it helps, that medicine. It keeps him civil and in control as long as I don't ask him to sit a minute and talk with me. If I do, he is tense, angry, ready to spring. Leaning toward me, glaring, he shakes his finger in my face.

"I'll sue you all. You keep me from my work. I'll lose all my contacts. You stole my computer. Now I can't run my business. I'm rich, no nickel-and-dime punk. You don't know it, but my lawyer is here, disguised and watching this all go down. I have a scanner in my phone. I have one in my contact lens. I can tell where the cameras are. I can tell when you're lying. I can tell."

This is my company for the long holiday weekend as I go about my job as a psychiatric nurse in a large county hospital.

My job of door locker
>	gate keeper
>	enforcer
>	rule maker
>	sex police
>	censor

My job as pill pusher
>	narcotics monitor
>	agent of darkness
>	agent of light

My job of hand holder
>	reassurer
>	a listening ear
>	a helping hand
>	a detector sniffing out alcohol breath and cigarette
>		smoke
>	sniffing out dirty shoes, fouled clothing

My license says registered nurse. They taught me none of this at nursing school. The sign above our ward entrance says "Psychiatric Unit," but some people call it the bug house. The hardest job is to be the door locker, the person with the key. I let people in and I let people out. I prevent escape. I confine, I restrain. It doesn't matter that it's for the patient's good, that the courts decree it, the doctors prescribe it, the illness requires it.

I lock up a person's belongings. Items that can be weapons. "Sharps," we call them.

>	car keys
>	aerosol containers
>	glass bottles, glass vases
>	mirrors
>	knives and scissors and razors and bottle openers
>	belts and shoe laces
>	picture glass
>	bags with straps, purses with straps
>	coffee cups

Not everything we lock away is sharp. Some are formless and clinging. We take away plastic bags, knot and discard them. "I'm sorry," I say. "You can't keep this. It'll be behind the desk. It's a safety rule."

Patients don't believe me. They are angry about the rules, that they can be told what they can and can't do, when they can smoke, where they can go, what they can wear and say. Some slam the desk with their hands. They shout things like, "It's a free world. I have my rights."

So I lock the doors, and I open the doors. I do what I can, as I can, and I pray for forgiveness for all the unconscious cruelties inflicted on these people confined behind the doors which, at the end of eight hours, I unlock, walk through, and leave behind.

Nursing 101: Pediatric Rotation

ANDREA VLAHAKIS *Woodbury, Connecticut*

I was
a student and he
was three.
He had burns
on the right side of his face —
the result
of his mother's love
when she'd tied him
to the blazing radiator to
sleep for the night.
I raged inside, but
he smiled at me,
the smile of angels.
I've carried this smile
in my pocket
for thirty-two years —
it rattles around, nudges me,
and opens up the path
my weariness
overgrows in.

Sixteen Standing Hours

FAITH VROMAN *Houtzdale, Pennsylvania*

For years I looked into the face of life and death,
sometimes for 16 standing hours at a time.
Tell me, world, that this was not important!
That sales quotas or power lunches require finer honed skills,
that briefcases carry data more important than a chest rising
    with breath.

Morning report was a litany of human horror,
the wait to hear our assignments
like awaiting the bullet in Russian Roulette.
We heard the gradients of life — survived one day, two days,
permanently brain damaged, terminal, no code.
The sword of Damocles was the "transfer out" leaving a now-
    empty bed.

Sometimes the bed was already reserved
for a high risk post-op fresh from major surgery
or the floor patient turned sour for any one of twenty reasons —
even the "stable" could arrest at any moment.

We drank in this tension with our morning coffee,
maybe the only break in our day —
forget food or rest or going to the bathroom.

Now I watch TV commercials, the importance of fiscal crisis,
    crucial it be solved,
feel the twist of a grimace at such pompous silliness.
You want to talk about crisis?
Let's talk six minutes, life or brain death,
then I'll look you in the eye.

Shots

BELLE WARING *Hyattsville, Maryland*

Three nurses to hold him, this four-year-old who kicks me
crazy in the belly — six months pregnant but *ha!*
I've got the needle — the Measles-Mumps-Rubella.
Child, it stings like hell.

Listen to me, my little immunized enemy —
I'll take a bruise from you
before I'll see another kid like the one carried through the clinic
    doors
at the end of shift in his father's arms, seizing
seizing
The father's shirt is
black with sweat
is praying in Mexican

grand mal, I try to get a line in, Mother of God, intractable
Get him over to St. Luke's

but in the ambulance, he codes and then, in the ER
with the furious swirl of personnel, crash cart rumbling up,
    curtains
snatched to shield him from the drive-bys and the drunks,
the boy expired.
Measles encephalitis.
He never got his shots.

So walk out, dark blonde, into the sun that will scald you red
and bleach your hair to tungsten burning, drive the dusty valley
    smacked with
irrigated fields. Bad counterfeit. Too green.

His young bones green, unripe, *gronjo*
from the old Teutonic root —

Green. Untrained. Green. Freshly killed.
His young bones green and full of marrow.

Green at work there in the rows, hands stretched out to pick a
beefsteak tomato at the end of season when they strip the plants
    clean
whether the fruit is ripe or not.

The Forgery

BELLE WARING *Hyattsville, Maryland*

— For uncrossmatched blood, the doctor must sign.

I said, It's for a baby! Stabbed in utero! *I'll* sign for the doctor.

— You mean *forge* it? Forget it.

The woman behind the blood bank counter then tapped on the
page with her index finger, with her salon-painted nail, tuff as an
escutcheon — tiny gold griffin on a field of carmine. O she had a
haughty eye.

— *Physician's* signature, she said.

— Where's your supervisor?

— I *am* the supervisor. And I'm not losing my job 'cause a *you.*

And since no pity would move her, nor rank, nor threat, and a
legal signature meant lost minutes, and since the baby was
preemie, the baby was shocky, and it was four in the morning,
gall of the night, I saw fit to go crazy.

— *Lose your job? Who'd want it?* I got two babies up there on *vents*
already, and now *this* one, *surprise!* The mother walks into the

ER, collapses, with multiple stab wounds, belly fulla blood, but when they take her to the OR and open her up *there's this twenty-eight-week fetus inside*. So they STAT-page us and the shit hits — *OK?* But you know why I like it? You get an admission, that crazy first hour, everybody works together, everybody helps you out, and you reach a point — not out of the woods, but you're getting there, *you feel it* — and somebody cracks a joke. You look up — you all laugh. *That* moment. *Help me*, I said.

She turned her back. Walked away. On the wall, someone had stuck a poster:

IT HAS COME TO THE ATTENTION OF THE MANAGEMENT THAT EMPLOYEES EXPIRING ON THE JOB ARE FAILING TO FALL DOWN. ANYONE WHO REMAINS DEAD IN AN UPRIGHT POSITION WILL BE DROPPED FROM THE PAYROLL.

Then she was back. Plunked down two pints of blood.

— Sign, she said.

So I signed, I forged, I grabbed the two units, uncrossmatched blood, color of garnets, color of beets, hugged the blood to my chest and I ran all three flights and I ran, never tired, the talker, the forger, I ran with the gorgeous, ran with the anonymous, ran with cold dark blood.

It Was My First Nursing Job

BELLE WARING *Hyattsville, Maryland*

and I was stupid in it. I thought a doctor would not be unkind.
One wouldn't wait for a laboring woman to dilate to ten cm.

He'd brace one hand up his patient's vagina,
clamp the other on her pregnant belly, and force the fetus

through an eight-centimeter cervix.
She tore, of course. Bled.

Stellate lacerations extend from the cervix
like an asterisk. The staff nurses stormed and hissed

but the head nurse shrugged, *He doesn't like to wait around.*
No other doctor witnessed what he did. The man was an elder

in his church. He chattered and smiled broadly as he worked.
He wore the biggest gloves we could stock.

It was my first real job and I was scared in it.
One night a patient of his was admitted

bleeding. The charge nurse said, *He won't rip her.*
You take this one.

So I took her.
She quickly delivered a dead baby boy.

Not long dead — you could tell by the skin, intact.
But long enough.

When I wrapped him in a blanket, the doctor flipped open the
cover
to let the mother view the body, according to custom.

The baby lay beside her.
He lay stretched out and still.

What a pity, the doctor said.
He seized the baby's penis between his own forefinger and
  thumb.

It was the first time I had ever seen a male not circumcised
and I was taken aback by the beauty of it.

Look, said the doctor, *a little boy. Just what we wanted.*
His hand, huge on the child, held the penis as if he'd found

a love charm hidden in his grandmother's linen.
And then he dropped it.

The mother didn't make a sound.
When the doctor left, she said to me in a far flat voice

I called and told him I was bleeding bad.
He told me not to worry.

I don't remember what I said. Just that
when I escorted her husband from the lobby

the doctor had already gone home. The new father followed me
with a joyful strut. I thought *Sweet Jesus Christ*

— *Did the doctor speak to you?*
— *No ma'am*, the father said.

I said quick-as-I-could-so-I-wouldn't-have-to-think—
The baby didn't make it.

The man doubled over. I told him all wrong.
I would do it all over again.

Say—
Please sir. Sit down. I'm so very sorry to tell you —

No. It's been sixteen years.
I would say, *I am your witness*.

No. I have never told the whole truth.
Forgive me.

It was my first job
and I was lost in it.

Stuff I Learned in Nursing School

ANNE WEBSTER *Atlanta, Georgia*

to say all the forbidden words:
goddamn, hellfire, fuck, shit,
to live in a tiny room with two other girls,
to drink red wine, Cuba libres,
to smoke cigarettes, to French inhale, French kiss —
to swab down eight bodies, make eight beds
at a fast trot, dizzy from not enough sleep
the head nurse yelling like a drill sergeant
before running off to three hours of class,
to learn how to poke needles in oranges,
in my roommates, to learn which hole for the enema,
which for the catheter, to stand when some asshole
doctor ambles in, all hands — like the one
we call Molest Me Gillespie —
to kiss some intern, me all over him,
like a tabby cat on fire,
then night duty, helping to catch greasy babies,
the gush of blood missing the bucket
I have to swab along with the clotted forceps —
to keep arm distance from old men's
pinching paws, to flip the sheet over
a show-off's wrinkled weenie,
to scrub for surgery, holding my hands
like the holy mother, to duck when I hand
some hungover surgeon the wrong instrument
and the whole tray comes flying at me,
to stifle gags at clouds of stink,
wiping shit-ooze from a withered butt,
or cleaning a bubbly mass, cancer that used
to be pink skin, to hold my face flat,
even smile, while I'm screaming inside,
looking at throbbing guts in an open belly,
to have some MD come at me, mad dog crazy,
snarling, when his patient goes bad,

for the whole world to treat me like a maid
when I've just watched someone's father die,
all of the above my ticket to punching
a time clock at a job that gives me
a bad back, varicose veins, medical liability,
work that makes friends think that they can say
any damn thing about their bodies
or that I really want to see their hairy scars,
and, yes, yes, to have a new patient say,
"Oh, you are *that* Anne. My neighbor still
talks about you, how you helped him
get through that terrible time."

Doppelganger

ANNE WEBSTER *Atlanta, Georgia*

I'm here to tell you it's not that easy being
two people at once. The nurse that I am nods,
noting symptoms. Yes, bone marrow suppression,
pneumonia, left ventricular hypertrophy
indicate a poor prognosis. As the patient,
short of breath, head split by bolts of pain,
I push the call button, count minutes until
a frazzled woman with a clipboard rushes in,
only to wait again for the pill, the relief.
The other nurses, the doctors, know I'm
a member of the club. We talk critical
platelet counts, rocketing hypertension.
Alone, I dial the automated report number.
*Webster, Anne: today's chest film shows
increased infiltrates of pneumonia.*
Pus boils in needle sticks; my fever spikes.
Is this the fatal infection? I've seen it all
too many times to think I should be spared.

Yet the woman that is me weeps for the man
she would leave, the shining years left, for
grandchildren who will grow up without her,
even as the nurse in me notes vital signs, tallies
figures in the chart, numbers in the red zone.

Smile! You're in a Nursing Home

MARY WENTZ *St. Louis, Missouri*

"Mary Wentz to the dining room. Mary Wentz." The summons on the intercom became more insistent as I hurried down the hall. In the center of the dining room the fountain splashed, its tiled bottom glittered with tossed coins. Ethel stood there, dripping wet, soup ladle in hand.

"How did your dress get so wet?" I asked. She gave me her practiced innocent look.

"The laundry forgot to put it in the dryer."

I laughed, because Ethel wasn't delusional. At eighty-two, she was as clearheaded and quick-witted as she was light-fingered. Diving for coins wasn't a sport but a business enterprise. She'd wrap the pennies in silver foil in the hope — always unfounded — that the vending machine would accept them as dimes. Ethel and I had laughed together before. A few weeks ago, I'd mysteriously lost the Scotch tape and the notepad from my desk and found them, not so mysteriously, in Ethel's nightstand.

"Why would you ever want to work in a nursing home?" other nurses ask, unable to believe it's my choice. They assume that I just can't cut it in the hot spots: the controlled chaos of the ER, the life-and-death drama of the OR, the organized intensity of a big city hospital.

But I've been there, done that.

I've worked neonatal ICU at a children's hospital, rejoicing when a two-pound preemie graduated to the Well Room, no longer dependent on a machine to sustain his wispy breaths. I've worked the med-surg floor at a general hospital where I saw a little of everything and learned a lot.

But I didn't laugh much until I began working at a nursing home.

Unlike hospital patients who come and go in days or weeks, my women — usually thirty-four of a thirty-eight bed division are women — come here to live and, almost always, to die. Because we're together for months or years, we get to know each other. I know that Ethel has a son, a successful businessman who's sometimes as embarrassed by his mother's pranks as she is proud of him. When he visits, she leads him all around the floor, into the dining room and the parlor, into the business offices, introducing him over and over again.

I know that Anna stashes plums in her drawer until fruit flies swarm because she can't escape her memories of the Depression years, when money was scarce and fresh fruit a rare treat. I know that Georgia hoards unused Styrofoam cups and that Eva still remembers the daughter she lost. I come to know my patients' burdens and problems as well as their joys, their laughter. They laughed as girls, as young women — they mustn't stop laughing now.

In the haste and hustle of the hospital, we'd refer to patients in a sort of verbal shorthand: "the gallbladder in room three"; "the thyroid in room four-ten." But in a nursing home, the patient in four-ten has a name, a history, a life. Here where I work her name is Lily. Once she sang at a café on the south side of Chicago; now, at our singalongs, she's a solo act, a star. She ran out of stage makeup long ago, so when she turns up with thick, wide-streaked eyebrows and Magic Marker royal blue smudged across her eyelids, she laughs at her ingenuity, and so do I.

In room four-eleven there's Birdie, a little Irish woman stooped from decades of factory work. She doesn't laugh easily, but roars when she hears a good joke. Margaret, in four-fifteen, was a seamstress, once the owner of a dress shop in the city.

Here, the residents have reached an age when the past might seem irrelevant, the future limited and uncertain — so we're especially careful to appreciate the moment. I first realized that good nursing care is *in* the small moment, in the details, when I was a nurses' aide thirty years ago. In those days bedpans were metal, and cold. When I lifted patients onto them, they'd wince. So I began warming the bedpans. Now, when I'm in charge on a Sunday, it's "fingernail day," when every hand is inspected and whoever needs a manicure gets one. If a ninety-year-old has long, hanging-down hair, I offer a crisp new haircut; she might even say she feels pretty again.

Talking to patients is honoring the moment too; something as simple as small talk can make a large difference. A resident who won't eat when a nurse stands over her insisting *You must eat!* will clean her plate if I sit with her at the table and chat. "Do you think it's going to rain?" I might ask. "Where did you find that lovely blouse?"

When I worked with premature babies, I held them, cuddled them, sang to them, always fearful they might die. In the nursing home, I hold hands and give comfort too, but I don't fear the deaths of my patients, because *they* don't. I remember only one woman who seemed afraid to die. She had a tight, fixed stare that I couldn't smooth away. But the dozens of others who have died, occasionally in my arms, were ready. They told me so.

Once someone said to me *You must be very cold and hard hearted to be able to watch people die.* I tried to explain that we nurses can't just break down and wring our hands and cry when our patients are dying; that would be failing them. We have to hold their hands and touch them and whisper that it's all right. Because it is. My work in a nursing home has made me aware of the confluent arc of our lives. Once this was a vague intellectual concept for me; now I understand in a personal and truly liberating way.

One bright morning when an aide and I were making morning rounds, Ethel didn't wake up. I followed protocol. I called another nurse to confirm. I called the doctor. I called her son. I called the mortuary. I emptied Ethel's closet, folded her clothes, and put them in a shopping bag. I opened her nightstand drawer, took out her comb and toothpaste and found, under her handkerchiefs, the ballpoint pen I'd been missing.

Then I laughed out loud.

Neonatal ICU

LEIGH WILKERSON *Burnsville, North Carolina*

Surely there are poems hidden here. Surely
the steady pump of the ventilator, the electric

pulse of a heart monitor seem noble enough,
saving minute lives with inhuman precision,

valiant machines whose beauty still fails
beside the barest black of any winter twig.

But the only poems here curl in warmers,
small beings already marked by chance,

like thin-skinned birds nesting
in rafters high above the factory floor.

Hands Beckoning

RICHARD YAKIMO *St. Louis, Missouri*

I accept his hand in mine, discretely assess the warmth of the skin, the blanching fingernail beds, the shape of the nails. We talk while I lightly stroke his hand, feeling the atrophied muscles, hot joints, skin as thin and crackly as the outermost layers of an onion. I hear wet breathing, wind whistling through pampas grass. I look into blue eyes, watery turquoise with darker flecks of blue and green, like the stone itself.

Despite frailty, this man craves life — yet releases life as smoothly as casting a dragonfly lure over a glassy lake. Holding his hand, my hand seems to hold a power I don't understand.

He tells me they call him Sam. His voice lilts with a three-quarter rhythm that compensates for his heart's ragged beat. He can't seem to remember my name, so he calls me *Boy* — my forty-three years no match for his additional fifty, even though he is the patient and I am the one nominally in charge. I smile at memories of patients who called me by their mothers' or sons' names. Some called me *doctor*; others called me *God*.

I feel hushed — I who have searched for God in cathedral, university, and sweat lodge — privileged to be in Sam's presence. With wit sharp as a tin can lid, he recalls the strip mines of Pickneyville, his prowess in commanding machinery that became his hand's extension — pickax to gasoline engine to a diesel like a brontosaurus, its long neck craned to scour vegetation from the slopes of man-hewn craters.

I slip through a wrinkle in time — the forty-three years I missed knowing him — to cradle his hands, comforted that he accepts my touch, preferring it to hard X ray table, needle sting, tangle of adhesive that tugs his fragile skin. If I could, I'd fill those mines with water, stock them with trout, offer Sam a line and pole instead of my cold stethoscope.

Afterword

JUDY SCHAEFER

"I never gave it a thought" was the response to most of my questions about danger, fear, and what motivated nurses in New Guinea in World War II.

I was talking to my friend, Captain Estelle "Stella" Pickle Sverchek. She is a hero. In the aftermath of September 11, 2001, her words reverberate with even more immediacy, more meaning. "I never gave it a thought" is what she said. Pearl Harbor motivated her. She had a job to do.

Many of us have been motivated by September 11. Most of us were at a distance and not at ground zero, but all our lives have been changed. The curious function of literature is to give both distance and reflection and, if the writer is fortunate, to give inspiration or at least a new perspective.

The nights were cold in New Guinea from time to time, and so were the Marines when they chided Stella for providing care for the Japanese prisoners of war — the enemy.

"The Marines were not too happy with me for taking care of them. They were just as young as our boys." But it was Stella's assignment, her duty. The Marines' chiding aside, camaraderie developed between the nurses and all members of the American military serving in New Guinea. The nurses hoarded cigarettes and beer for the purpose of barter. Get-togethers were held on a hill hidden by trees. Stella told me how these soldiers were more like family than her family back home. When she finally returned to the States, she missed them.

Nursing, the backbone of our health care system, has many such heroes: nurses like Stella; like Shulamith Cantor; like the 24/7 nurses we write about; like the nurse/writers who've contributed to this anthology; like all the nurses whose names you may never know — we are all called upon to provide care in situations of moral ambiguity, especially in today's high tech and multifaceted workplace. Often, nurses work overtime. Sometimes we are underappreciated. But we have the good fortune of working within a profession which mandates compassion and kindness.

These attributes are at the very core of our lives and at the center of our poems and stories. These attributes are why we are capable of such intensive caring. Thank you to the gentle, tough heroes of this book. Thank you, reader, for taking this journey with us.

Krystina Ahlman wrote her first poem at age fifteen after volunteering at
a local nursing home. At thirty, she graduated from Colby Saw-
yer College, summa cum laude, with dual degrees in nursing and
English/creative writing. She has published numerous poems in
small-press magazines.

Frances Murphy Araujo is a psychiatric clinical nurse who practices in
an emergency department in a hospital south of Boston. Her fic-
tion has appeared in *Kalliope*, *Lynx Eye*, *Reed Magazine*, *Washington
Square*, and other journals. Her work has received a Pushcart Prize
nomination.

Jane Bailey works as a nurse in Oregon. Recipient of poetry fellowships
from Oregon Literary Arts and the Oregon Arts Commission, her
work has appeared in *Prairie Schooner*, *Many Mountains Moving*,
Calyx, and in *Poetry Northwest*, which awarded her the Richard
Hugo Prize.

Carol Battaglia received her BSN from Loyola University and works in
Loyola's Medical Center. Author of three books, *Murmurs*, *Jagged
Rhythms*, and *Drifting among the Whales*, she attributes her success
to nursing instructors who encouraged her and continue to pro-
mote her work.

Andrea Lee Beliveau says that while her technical strengths have flow-
ered in several specialties, intimate connections with human be-
ings are the root of her career. She published *Behind the Scenes* in
2000, and in 2001 she launched a column, "Bedside Manners," in a
Canadian nephrology journal.

Lynn Bernardini graduated from nursing school in 1989 after a first ca-
reer as a statistical analyst for Winchester Firearms International
Division. She has worked in neonatal intensive care for fourteen
years. "Does This Date Mean Anything to You?" is her first pub-
lished piece.

Janet Bernichon now works in the field of addiction after more than
twenty-five years in critical care and emergency nursing. A widely
published poet, she says that changing from healthy caregiver to
cancer patient, at the least a very humbling experience, has made
her appreciate the importance of caring.

Hanne Dina Bernstein is an RN from Denmark, now living in Mas-
sachusetts. Her nursing experience includes intensive care, burn
unit, and oncology. She started writing poems about nursing a year
ago and is presently working on a book of fairy tales.

Kirstin Bortz has BA degrees in nursing and anthropology. Drawn to nursing by a strong interest in midwifery and in working overseas, she is currently a women's health educator in Brazil, helping women and youth to discover their own value and to better care for themselves and their families.

Geoffrey Bowe qualified as a nurse in 1983 and has spent the last sixteen years at the Medway Maritime Hospital in Kent, England. His poems have been published in the *Nursing Standard* and in *Between the Heartbeats: Poetry and Prose by Nurses*.

Ruth E. Brooks graduated from Harlem Hospital School of Nursing in 1960 and has worked in a wide variety of positions. Her work appeared in *Between the Heartbeats: Poetry and Prose by Nurses*, and her articles, book reviews, and prose have been published in the *American Journal of Nursing*.

Celia Brown trained as a nurse in England and obtained her master's degree from Dartmouth in 1981. She is the author of *Mending the Skies* and her work has appeared in numerous journals and anthologies. She has been a poet in the schools and was a Jenny McKean Fellow at George Washington University.

Jeanne Bryner graduated from Trumbull Memorial Hospital School of Nursing and from the Honors College of Kent State. Recipient of writing fellowships from Bucknell, the Ohio Arts Council, and the Wick Poetry Program at Kent State, she is the author of two poetry collections, *Breathless* and *Blind Horse*.

Teresa Campbell is Professor Emeritus of Nursing at San Francisco State University. She has published a variety of articles in nursing and non-nursing journals and magazines and is the author of *Life is an Adventure*.

Shulamith Cantor (1894–1979) graduated from the nursing school of the American University in Beirut and became the first Hebrew-speaking teacher at what is now the Henrietta Szold Hadassah-Hebrew University School of Nursing. After Israeli independence, she was appointed Director of Nursing Services for the Ministry of Health. Her memoir can be read at the American Jewish Historical Society (Hadassah Archives) in New York City.

Alice Capshaw has degrees in nursing and organizational behavior. She works as a float nurse covering medical-surgical units, psychiatry, homecare, discharge planning, and extended care. Her real loves are hospice and care of the elderly, which she considers spiritual experiences.

Marlene Cesar was born in Haiti and attended medical school in Bolivia; she then received an accounting degree in Chicago. After working for the Royal Canadian Mint and as a math teacher in Florida, she graduated from nursing school at Miami-Dade Community College and now works as a psych nurse. She's currently pursuing her MSN.

Robin Chard is a practicing perioperative nurse, a nursing instructor in a BSN program, and a part-time student in a doctoral nursing program. A frequent presenter at conferences, she has been writing poetry for several years, focusing on the world of nursing and on childhood memories.

Victoria May Collett is an OR nurse who writes novels and short stories. She has been published in the literary magazines *Inkwell*, *Lumina*, and *Edge City Review*. She holds a master of arts in writing from Manhattanville College in addition to her nursing credentials.

Cortney Davis, a nurse practitioner in women's health, is the author of *I Knew a Woman: the Experience of the Female Body* and of two poetry collections, *The Body Flute* and *Details of Flesh*. She has received an NEA Poetry Fellowship and two Connecticut Commission on the Arts Poetry Grants.

Theodore Deppe is the author of *Cape Clear: New and Selected Poems*, *Children of the Air*, and *The Wanderer King*. Recipient of NEA, Connecticut Commission on the Arts, and Massachusetts Cultural Council grants, he is poet-in-residence at the Poet's House, Donegal, Ireland.

Sandra Bishop Ebner works as a psychiatric case manager. Her poems have appeared in a variety of literary journals, and she teaches poetry to seventh graders as part of a grant-funded program. Her book, *The Space Between*, was published in 2000.

Terry Evans has been a nurse for half of her life. Married to a military man, she traveled and experienced many different facets of nursing before settling on labor and delivery and becoming a certified childbirth educator.

Maureen Tolman Flannery works with a plastic surgeon in Chicago. Her books include *Secret of the Rising Up: Poems of Mexico*, and *Remembered into Life*. She edited the anthology *Knowing Stones: Poems of Exotic Places*, and publishes widely.

Helen Trubek Glenn holds nursing degrees from Cornell University. Her poems have appeared in the *Nebraska Review*, *Spoon River Review*, *Poet Lore*, and numerous other journals and anthologies. Her poetry collection, *The Burden of the Story*, was a finalist for the Bluestem Award.

Chris Grant holds a BSN from Iowa Wesleyan College and an MSN and PhD in psychiatric mental health nursing from the University of

Pennsylvania. She maintains a private practice and provides expert testimony in court in the areas of sexual abuse, spousal violence, and rape.

Amy Haddad teaches ethics at Creighton University. Her poetry and short stories have been published in the *American Journal of Nursing*, *Fetishes*, the *Library Journal of Colorado Health Sciences Center*, and *Journal of Medical Humanities*. She is co-editor of *The Arduous Touch: Women's Voices in Health Care* (1999).

Pauline Hebert served with the Army Nurse Corps in Cu Chi, Vietnam, in 1968. Her poems have appeared in *From Both Sides Now: the Poetry of the Vietnam War and Its Aftermath*, *Rattle: Poetry for the 21st Century*, and also online at www.echonyc.com/~poets.

Nina Howes is a registered nurse and a political activist. For the past ten years, she has worked in an HIV clinic. She writes essays and collects oral histories and recently collaborated on an adaption of *Lysistrata* for a community theater.

Karen Howland believes that stories, song, and poetry are potent medicine. After becoming an RN, fascinated with the connection between health and creativity, she studied music at the Conservatory of Music and also completed her master's in creative writing. She facilitates women's writing circles in the Midwest.

Hilarie Jones has been an RN for seventeen years, an APRN for seven years, and a wordsmith for over forty. Oncology and hospice were her first nursing passions, and now she practices as a nurse practitioner in adult primary care.

Alyson Kennedy worked on a medical-surgical ward as a staff RN for eighteen years and left nursing in 2001 to pursue other career options. She writes poetry and short stories; this is her first publication.

Sue Klassen is a family nurse practitioner working in Nicaragua through the church development agency, Mennonite Central Committee. A graduate of the nursing program at University of Virginia, she has also worked in Mozambique and Washington, D.C.

Shirley Kobar practices at the General Clinical Research Center of the University of Colorado in Denver. Her poems have appeared in *American Journal of Nursing*, *Fetishes*, *Buffalo Bones*, and in *Between the Heartbeats: Poetry and Prose by Nurses*.

Joan Stack Kovach currently works as a nurse psychotherapist with expatriates in Budapest. She studied nursing at Georgetown University and Boston College, and writing at the University of Massachusetts William Joiner Center. When not in Hungary, she lives in Massachusetts.

Debra Kowalski says that it is important for her to dedicate her story, "Endurance and Faith," to nurses everywhere who work against impossible odds. She also thanks her husband, Robert, and her friend, Theodore Deppe, "both extraordinary nurses and writers whose faith in me has given my life meaning."

Scott Chisholm Lamont is a pediatric critical care nurse and flight nurse. Originally from Canada, he currently practices at the University of New Mexico Health Sciences Center. His short stories have been anthologized and his poetry has been read on CBC radio in Alberta. "Four Men, Sitting" is excerpted from a longer version of his poem by the same name.

Jeanne LeVasseur holds an MFA in writing from Vermont College, a PhD in nursing from the University of Connecticut, and currently teaches nursing at Quinnipiac University. Her poems have been published in *Yankee*, *Spoon River Poetry Review*, *Literature and Medicine*, *JAMA*, *Kansas Quarterly*, *Nimrod*, and other journals.

Patricia Maher is a nurse practitioner with Health Care for the Homeless in Cambridge, Massachusetts. She holds a BSN and MSN and is completing her MA in theology and pastoral ministry.

Veneta Masson is a nurse and writer living in Washington, D.C. *Ninth Street Notebook—Voice of a Nurse in the City*, a collection of short takes from her long career in nursing, won a Book of the Year Award from *American Journal of Nursing*. She continues to explore healing art in all its forms.

Elizabeth Keough McDonald considers herself a poet who happens to have training in nursing. Nursing is one of the many areas her poetry addresses. She says that nursing has honed her observational skills and put her in touch with a variety of emotions: "For these qualities, I am grateful to my profession."

Pamela Mitchell currently teaches writing at Adirondack Community College. A graduate of SUNY-Upstate Medical Center and of Goddard's MFA program, she has practiced nursing in neuropsychiatry and holistic health from New York to Seattle for twenty-five years.

Muriel Murch graduated from the Royal Surrey County Hospital in Guilford, England, and obtained her BSN from San Francisco State University. Her book, *Journey in the Middle of the Road*, was published in 1995.

Madeleine Mysko is an RN in a retirement community and also teaches creative writing. A graduate of the writing seminars of Johns Hopkins University, her work has appeared in *Hudson Review*, *Shenandoah*, *The Christian Century*, and other journals. Her first novel is based on her experiences as an Army nurse during the Vietnam War.

Carol Nachtrab received her RN degree from Lima Memorial Hospital and served from 1970 to 1972 as a captain in the Army Nurse Corps in Vietnam. After working in Wyoming and Maryland, she is now a patient and community educator at Henry County Hospital in Napoleon, Ohio.

Miriam Bruning Payne is a neonatal intensive care nurse at West Boca Medical Center where she specializes in working with Spanish-speaking families. Her poems have been published in *Coastlines*, and she lives in Boca Raton.

Christine Rahn retired after a thirty-five year career that included staff and management positions and returned to the University of Washington for her BA. She says, "I took creative writing classes so I could record the stories of my favorite patients. They taught me about living and dying with courage, patience, and dignity."

Geri Rosenzweig grew up in Ireland where she worked as an RN before coming to New York. Her books include *Under the Jasmine Moon*, *Half the Story*, and *White Sandals*. Her many writing honors include the Walt Whitman and Voices Israel awards.

Jo-Anne Rowley lives and works in Denver, Colorado. She has published poems in *Graces, Bless the Day, Bedside Prayers, Mediphors, Buffalo Bones*, and *Array*.

Judy Schaefer is co-editor of *Between the Heartbeats: Poetry and Prose by Nurses* and author of *Harvesting the Dew*. Her writing appears in *Academic Medicine, American Journal of Nursing, Journal of Medical Humanities, Lancet, Literature and Medicine*, and other publications. She lectures part time at Penn State University and also lectures widely in this country and abroad.

Paula Sergi is co-editor of *Boomer Girls: Poems by Women from the Baby Boom Generation* (University of Iowa Press). Her poems have appeared in *Crab Orchard Review, Spoon River Poetry Review, Primavera*, and other journals. She earned a BSN and MFA and received a Wisconsin Arts Board Artist Fellowship Award in 2001.

Jessica Shrader has been a medical-surgical nurse since her graduation in 1995. She enjoys the night shift—when patients can't sleep, she says, they offer unique insights into their lives. "Long-Term Companion" is her first publication.

Kelly Sievers is a nurse anesthetist. Her poem provided the title for *Between the Heartbeats: Poetry and Prose by Nurses*. Her poetry and fiction also appears in *Prairie Schooner, Seattle Review, Ellipsis, Writer's Forum, Hayden's Ferry Review, Descant, Other Voices, Wisconsin Academy Review*, and other journals.

Kathleen Walsh Spencer, a nurse practitioner, has published widely in *Ekphrasis*, the *Red Cedar Review*, *American Poetry Monthly*, *Mediphors*, *Inkwell*, the *MacGuffin*, and other journals. Editor of the *Plastic Surgical Nursing Journal*, she lives in metropolitan Detroit and has won numerous writing awards.

Constance Studer is author of *Prayer to a Purple God*. Her poems, fiction, essays, and translations have been widely published and anthologized. In addition to a diploma in nursing, she holds a BA in English Literature and an MA in writing. She has work forthcoming in *Kaleidoscope* and *American Journal of Nursing*.

Sallie Tisdale is the author of many books, most recently, *The Best Thing I Ever Tasted: the Secret of Food*. Her essays and articles have been widely published in magazines such as *Harper's*, *Elle*, and *Audubon*, and she is a columnist for the online magazine *Salon*.

Janet Tripp is a feminist, writer, journal teacher, and nurse whose life is synthesized on paper. She has edited a feminist journal, published essays and biographies and, as a parish nurse, written healing prayers and rituals.

Andrea Vlahakis is a certified IV nurse therapist who has worked in oncology, pediatrics, and acute care. Her poetry has been published in *Connecticut River Review*, *Comstock Review*, *Christian Science Review*, and other journals. She also publishes fiction and nonfiction for children and is currently working on two picture books.

Faith Vroman says that, after the usual med-surg, ICU, CCU, Recovery Room, and union organizing expenditure of energy, she quietly became a private duty nurse to an elderly woman: "Nineteen years of study, writing, exploring the inner landscapes." She now dances with senior citizens at an adult center, "finally peaceful, finally happy."

Belle Waring is the author of two poetry collections, *Refuge*, which won the Washington Prize, and *Dark Blonde*. Recipient of fellowships from the NEA, the D.C. Commission on the Arts, and the Fine Arts Work Center, she has taught creative writing at Children's Hospital in D.C.

Anne Webster retired from nursing to write. Her poems have appeared in *Southern Poetry Review*, *New York Quarterly*, and *Mediphors*. Her book, *In Sickness and in Health*, was a finalist for the Ashland Poetry Prize. She is currently writing a memoir, *A Second Choice Life*, about her nursing career.

Mary Wentz graduated from a diploma program at age fifty-three, becoming an RN after raising her family. A volunteer at Ronald McDonald House, she has spent most of her career at a geriatric center where she became Assistant Director of Nursing.

Leigh Wilkerson, RN, BSN, worked for five years in neonatal intensive care. She now works in adult critical care at a rural hospital in the mountains of North Carolina.

Richard Yakimo, MSN, RN, CS, is a doctoral student at Saint Louis University School of Nursing, focusing his research on the psychosocial care of the physically ill. His clinical background is in geropsychiatric nursing with special interest in memory impairment and end-of-life care.